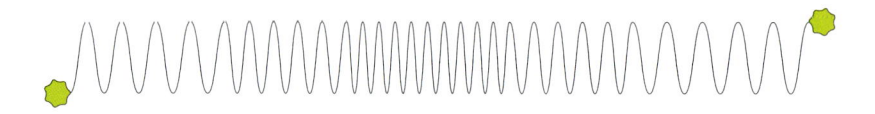

pedal culture

guitar effects pedals
as cultural artifacts

Ronald Light

Design by Megan Pai

Backbeat Books

Guilford, Connecticut

Backbeat Books

An imprint of Globe Pequot, the trade division of The Rowman & Littlefield Publishing Group, Inc.
4501 Forbes Blvd., Ste. 200
Lanham, MD 20706
www.rowman.com

Distributed by NATIONAL BOOK NETWORK

Copyright © 2022 Ronald Light

Photography by Jeff Spirer unless otherwise credited
Text by Ronald Light
Design by Megan Pai

The exhibition PedalCulture: The Guitar Effects Pedal as Cultural Artifact was organized and guest curated by Ronald Light in association with DESIGNSPACE, School of Design, San Francisco State University.

All rights reserved. No part of this book may be reproduced in any form or by any electronic or mechanical means, including information storage and retrieval systems, without written permission from the publisher, except by a reviewer who may quote passages in a review.

British Library Cataloguing in Publication Information available

Library of Congress Cataloging-in-Publication Data available

ISBN 978-1-4930-6079-5 (hardcover)
ISBN 978-1-4930-6080-1 (e-book)

♾️™ The paper used in this publication meets the minimum requirements of American National Standard for Information Sciences–Permanence of Paper for Printed Library Materials, ANSI/NISO Z39.48-1992

dal   culture

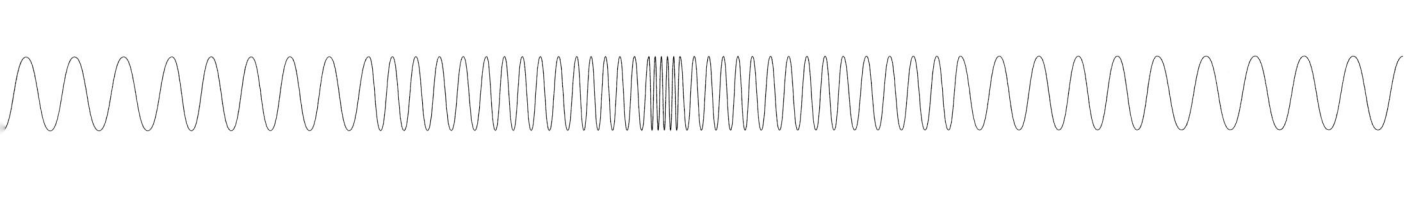

v

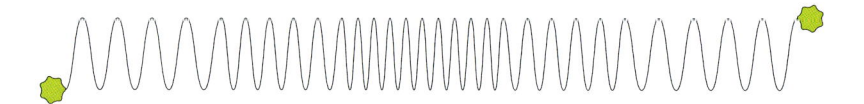

About PedalCulture...

PedalCulture was an insanely enlightening interactive exhibition that deserves to live on as catalogue. It delivers tons of practical information about guitar pedals while bringing personality to the presentations and a funky flare to text descriptions. I was shocked at how many wonderfully weird pedals - detailing the hip mystique of boutique stompboxes - Ron was able to secure for the exhibition. The whole affair was a worthy tribute to the ingenious lab cats that conjure wildly unique creative tools, and the players that use them to transform the sonic landscape into evermore-outrageous terrain. Everyone who loves otherworldly sounds and artisan craftsmanship will appreciate a playful dose of PedalCulture.

-Jimmy Leslie
Frets Editor at *Guitar Player*

I am amazed at what the world of Guitar Effects Pedals has become. The sheer scale and breadth of the industry today is beyond anything I could have foreseen three decades ago. There was little hint in the early 1990's that guitar effects pedals were on a path to creating a unique culture all their own, or even that they might become an entirely new medium for genuine artistic expression beyond their sonic functions. I was honored to have my work included in this very special exhibition, and to see effects pedals displayed to the public in this way as a form of high art all onto themselves I think was a spectacle long overdue. I do wonder if museums of the future will have effects pedals in their collections, and will they regularly display them as we display paintings and sculptures today? I can only guess - but the PedalCulture exhibition is certainly a good start.

-Fran Blanche
Frantone Electronics

Preface

Preface

I first picked up a guitar in 2014 at age 65 with three objectives in mind: First, to learn to strum the Stones' "You Can't Always Get What You Want;" second, to enjoy learning to play along with my best childhood friend who'd suggested we both buy guitars (lap guitars, at that); and finally, to attempt to stave off the ill effects of advancing age (death, the illest of them all) by attempting to climb the Mount Everest of feats - learning to play a musical instrument - and thus force my brain to plant and harvest a large new crop of white matter. By way of a status report six years later: I've learned that "You Can't Always Get What You Want" literally happens to be true - the song is not amenable to strumming, but to fingerpicking. My friend has become an accomplished and sought after blues harmonica player. And as for white matter (the neurotransmitters of the brain), I remain alive, alert and able to practice guitar, so I guess things aren't going too badly.

What I didn't expect - in fact, a world I didn't know even existed - was that I would become consumed by guitar gear (i.e. a "gearhead") obsessively lusting after new guitars, amplifiers and guitar effects pedals. For some reason unbeknown to most people, the affliction known as "gear acquisition syndrome" (GAS, for short) is most acute with guitar effects pedals, and a large and highly consuming commercial world has grown up because of it. In short, I bought my first effects pedal. And then, another. And so on.

At some point I guess a degree of self-awareness must have set in, and I became intensely curious about the social meaning and symbolic associations of guitar effects pedals in the cultural and cognitive worlds of obsessive guitar fandom. Besides, thinking about the place of guitar effects in "guitar culture" fueled my desire and fanned the flames of obsession over the pedals themselves. Encouraging yourself to think about what you can't stop thinking about is a symbiosis made in heaven, I reasoned. In truth, the first point of fascination for me with stompbox culture was this: With the exception of the aboriginal Aranta tribe and maybe the most devout of Catholics, no other people on this planet attribute so much mana (supernatural power) to inanimate objects as do rock and roll guitarists. I noticed a pervasive and near-compulsive attraction to certain effects boxes that had been associated historically (and now, expressed in the realm of legend) with the likes of Jimi Hendrix, Stevie Ray Vaughn, David Gilmour - really, all the guitar biggies of a certain era. The anthropological and mythological aspects of this were just too juicy to ignore. And so I didn't.

Since it was the special power emanating from these material entities that was the source of my fascination, it became immediately obvious that an exhibition of road worn guitar effects pedals was the best way to showcase the devices as power objects and bring the phenomenon to wider, public attention. Once bitten by the bug of an idea, my agenda was twofold: First, to begin to develop the idea into a proposal explaining what the shape - conceptually, and thematically - of an exhibition might look like, and next to begin thinking about an appropriate venue - a gallery - in which to stage the exhibition. When I read about the planned opening of the Design Gallery - later christened DESIGNSPACE - in the School of Design at San Francisco State

University I had a strong feeling of this place where it might all come together. All arrows seemed to point in that direction, and the prospect of exhibiting in a gallery of design would strongly inform my curatorial focus. The most exciting thing of all was the prospect of bringing students into the equation: As an outside curator pitching an unsolicited proposal I felt it essential that my plan be an invitation for students to dive into an enriching educational experience of real-world learning. Albeit unsolicited, my proposal could be a win-win for the university, for students and for myself. In short, it might prevail - and so it did!

At the beginning of 2017, gallery director (and associate professor of design) Joshua Singer signed off on a plan for my developing an exhibition under the auspices of the School's gallery. I offered to secure funding; to organize and curate the exhibition in all its aspects; to source all necessary objects (guitar pedals) for display; to perform public outreach and publicity - in short, to do everything necessary to ensure an appropriate level of curatorship due a university gallery of applied arts and technology. Thousands of hours of time would be required to do the requisite research and interpretive work in addition to the many logistical tasks necessary for mounting the exhibition. The only problem was that so much of the gallery's schedule already had been booked, so the pedal exhibition would need to open in eight months' time. Nothing like a tight schedule to get things going!

In spring, 2017 I was introduced to the then students of Design 628 - Design Gallery: Exhibitions and Communications, where I went to recruit their interest (and, with luck, ignite their passion) in developing an exhibition topic dear to me, if not yet to anyone else. In scope, students would design the gallery show itself in addition to producing all collateral materials such as a logo, a poster, text and signage, etc. Moreover, students would be expected to physically install the exhibition and manage gallery proceedings during the several weeks of the show's duration. Unfortunately, the spring semester was ending soon, and all but four students moving on into the world of their adult lives before the beginning of the following term. Over the summer several students (most notably, Lizzy Johnson) met with me weekly and dived into various exercises in design development for the show, earning independent study credits along the way. These efforts resulted in a well formulated pop art inspired aesthetic and the first iterations of a logo and poster that would guide and inform design development for all aspects of the exhibition to follow.

The fall semester class of DES 628 already had plenty on its plate with a full schedule of exhibitions almost from the start of the term. Then, some eight weeks before the October 31 opening, the class turned its full attention to the large scope of responsibility for conceiving, designing and producing the "look" of PedalCulture in its myriad forms and media. Students voiced concerns about the scope of the exhibition, and about content, too. As yet unfamiliar with the world of guitar effects, they were adamant there be more in the way of background content, such as an exhibit that explained how a pedal actually worked, and an opportunity for visitors to hear an effect's sonic signature. They wanted there to be a display of guitar effects history, too. Bending to these requests allowed for more direct student involve-

Preface

pedal culture

Curator's documentation

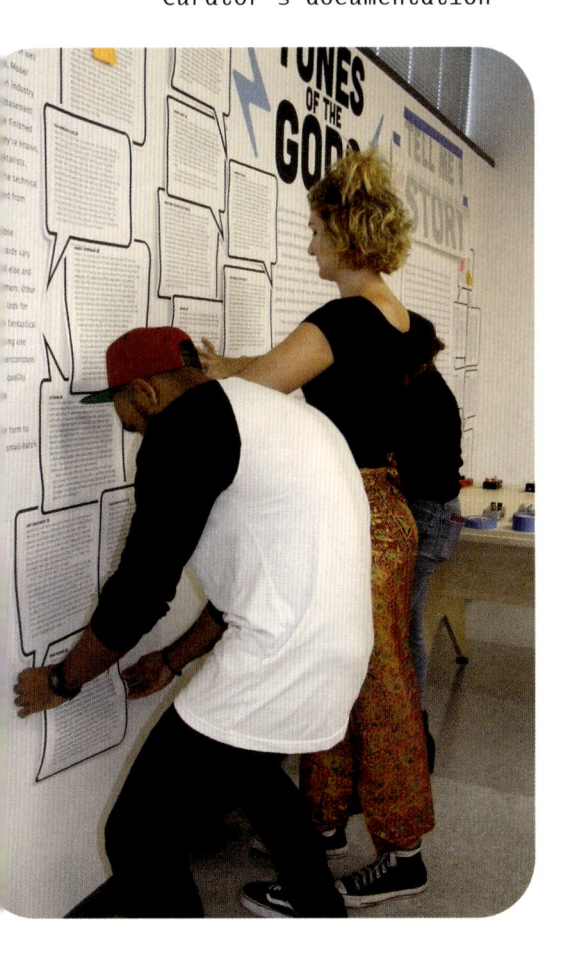

ment in educational displays, and several of the more didactic exhibits are wholly indebted to student input.

Around the same time, I looked up and couldn't help but notice I was directly in the path of a fast moving freight train heading my way: Nothing but deadlines between the current moment and the show's opening, and far too few hours (even with sleepless nights) to accomplish what needed doing. I made several attempts to recruit a paid student assistant from among the university's student body, but nobody remained beyond an initial meeting. I must have been a terror! Oh well, just work harder…

Design 628 began working overtime, too. Two students helped intake, organize and catalog the 63 guitar effects pedals arriving by mail from nine different countries and 38 different suppliers. Other students took turns creating the highly expressive and colorful rock star posters that would adorn the Rock It 8/8 wall of music, taking inspiration from the psychedelic posters of the 1960s. The exhibition would require a unique logo, large swatches of vinyl display type and dense passages of text outlined in cartoon dialog bubbles, all designed, typeset, cutout and wall mounted for each

Preface

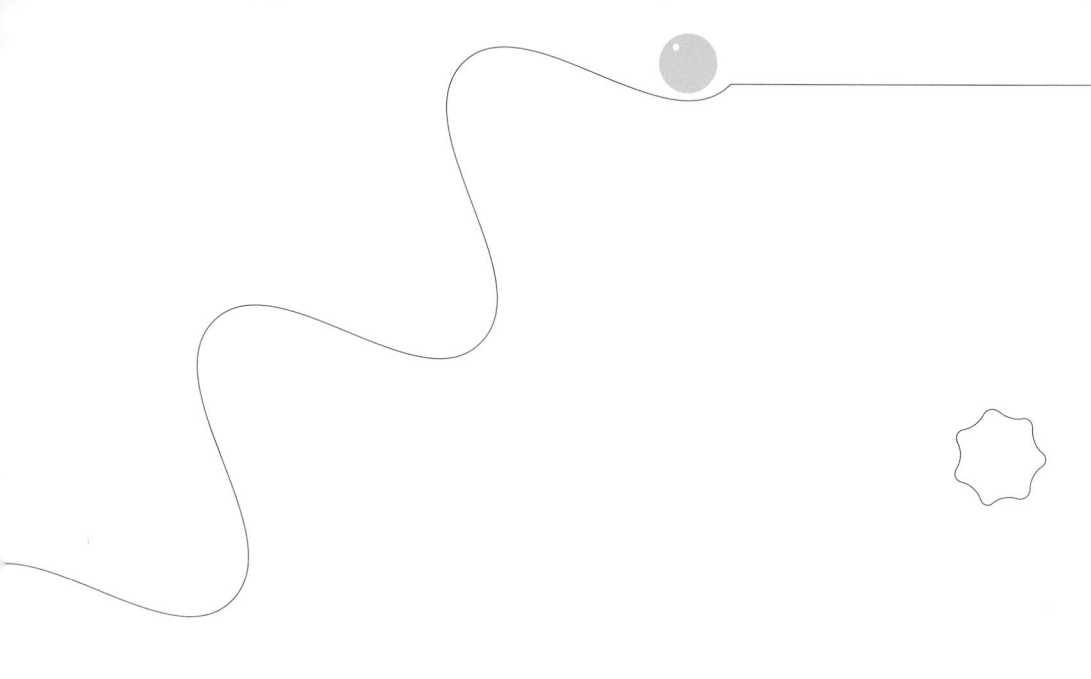

exhibit. Several displays were conceived as three-dimensional art installations, and lots of thought and work went into creating the "peep show" curtain for Fuzzy Muff Petting Zoo, the Holy Wahcamoly decorative display and the interactive Hall of Fame 2 working pedal demonstration. Three new exhibit cases had to be built in-house in time for installation of display objects. The PedalCulture logo was finalized, and a poster backed with descriptive program sent out for printing. Finally, 480 bags of tortilla chips donated by Casa Sanchez landed at the School's curbside address, because how can you have a Holy Wahcamoly pedal exhibit without a few chips for dipping? Rising well above the call of duty to class and lab time and guided throughout by Professor Singer, the students of Design 628 (with the assistance of a few outside agitators, friends of the curator) transformed DESIGNSPACE into "PedalCulture" in time for a November 2 opening reception and live performance incorporating as many different sonic effects as guitar soloist Jimmy Leslie could string together on two pedalboards.

What you hold in your hands (or see gleaming from the likes of an LCD or LED display) is testament to the boundless inspiration, the tireless effort and, ultimately, the overwhelming generosity of everyone involved in PedalCulture. I hope you find perusing this catalog a genuinely worthwhile and enriching experience and maybe amusing, too, with some unexpected and cheeky commentary. Comments, questions and general inquiries from you, the reader, are welcome.

—RL

pedal culture

Professor Singer would proclaim, "this is definitely the most ambitious show we've had."

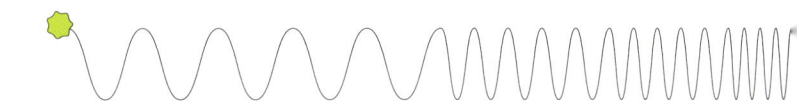

Photo by Kerri Leslie

Preface

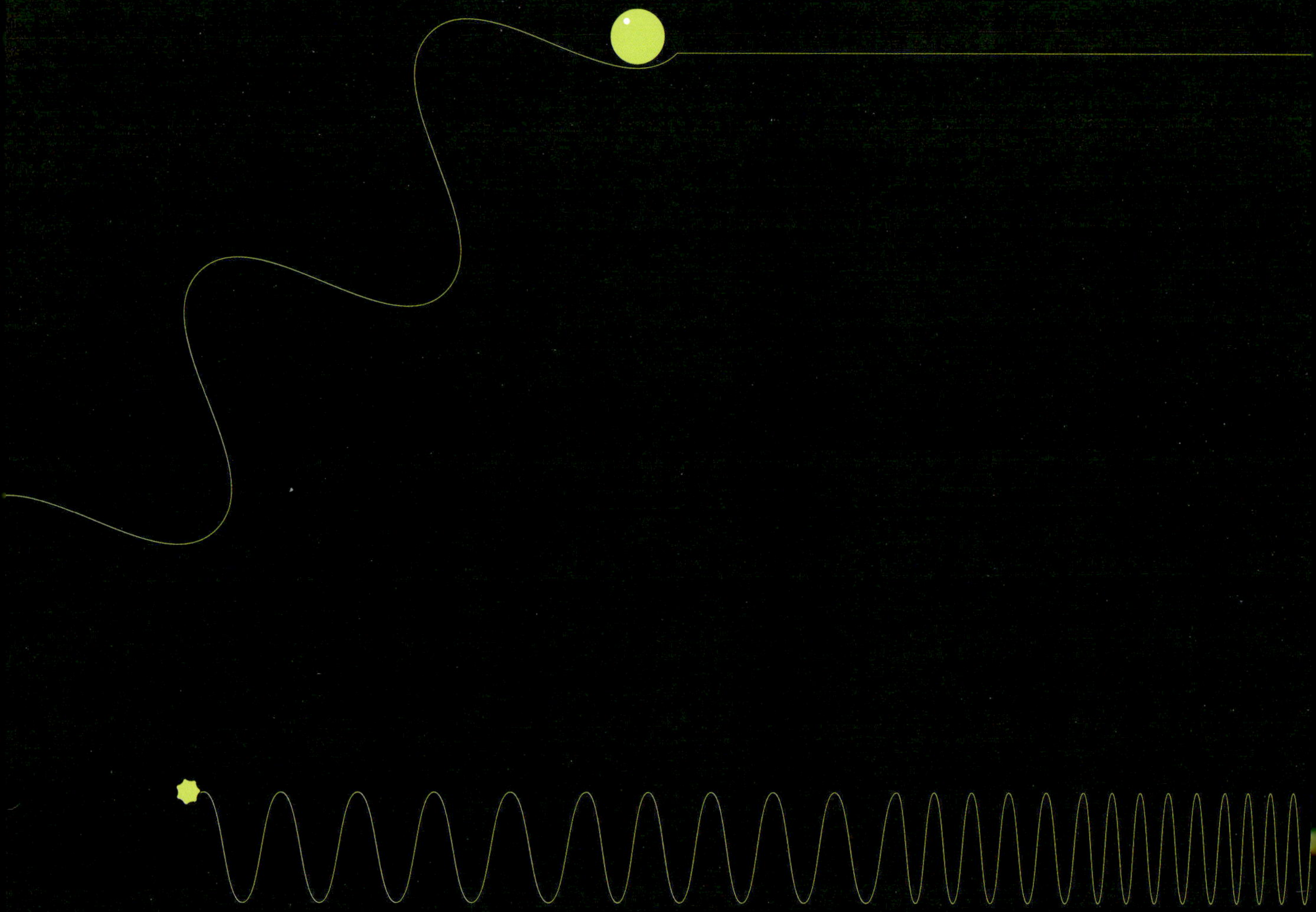

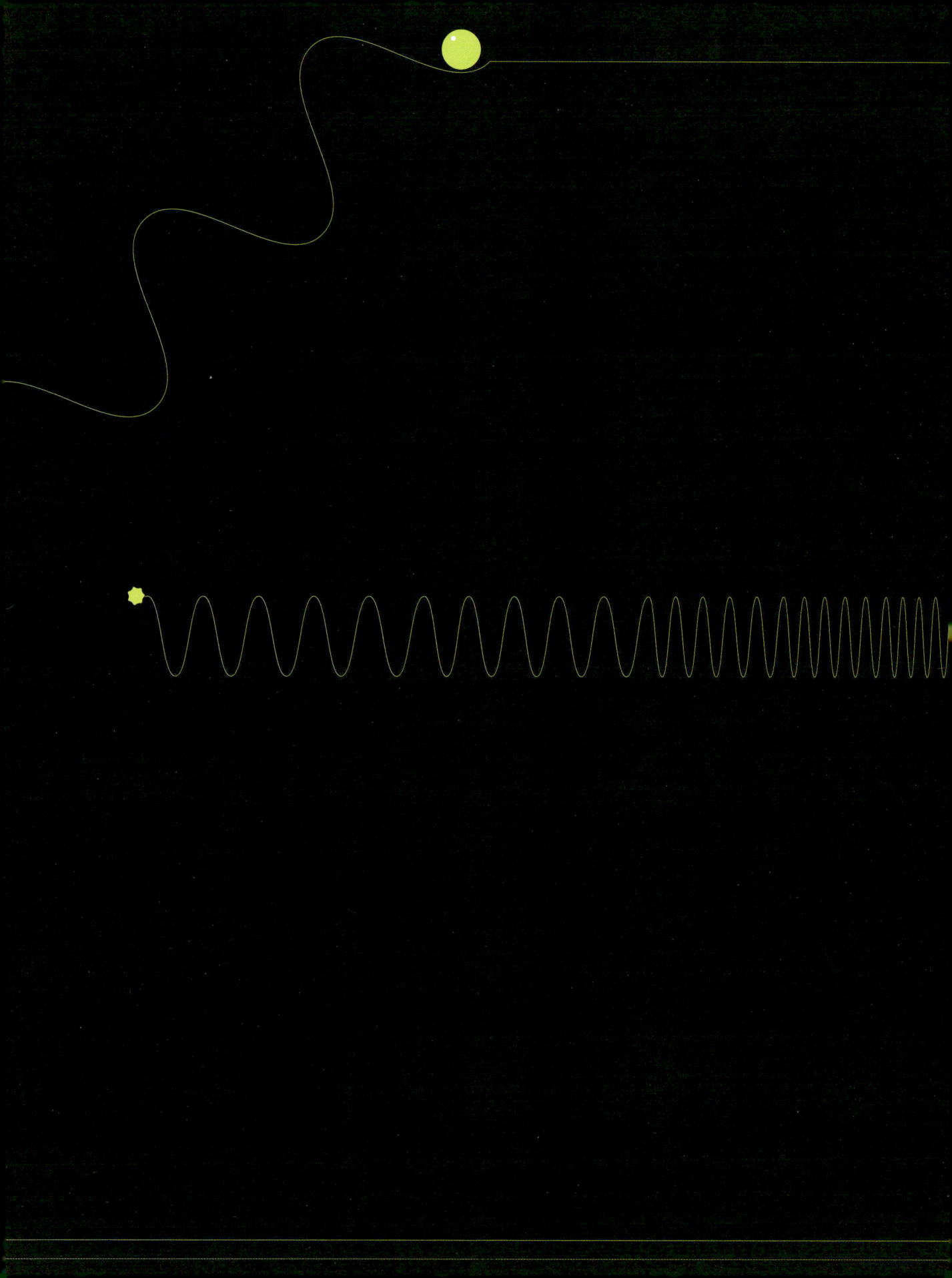

THE GUITAR EFFECTS PEDAL AS CULTURAL ARTIFACT
PEDAL CULTURE
DESIGNSPACE
OCT 31-NOV 17!
SAN FRANCISCO
STATE UNIVERSITY
OPENING RECEPTION!
THURSDAY, NOVEMBER 2
4:00 - 7:00 PM
PERFORMANCE &
PANEL DISCUSSION!
FOR ADDITIONAL INFORMATION:
PEDALCULTURE@ATT.NET
-OR- JSINGER@SFSU.EDU

Hail, hail rock 'n' roll!

Introduction

pedal culture

The Culture of Guitar Effects Pedals

Guitar Effects Pedals in the Culture

When Chuck Berry's mythical Johnny B. Goode picked up his axe and brought rock 'n' roll to the postwar teenage masses, rock's exuberance and swagger propelled an emergent musical form beyond style, beyond substance, to something more closely resembling a cultural shift. Youth everywhere heard the siren sound of a wailing electric guitar plugged into a searing overdriven amplifier - thus ensuring that music would never be the same and, perhaps more importantly, would popular culture.

As rock 'n' roll became the dominant form of popular music in America, recording technology rapidly evolved to meet and greet the raucous upstart with a palette of newly conceived sonic effects for music production and recording. By the early 1960s there were portable devices for producing reverb, echo, tremolo, vibrato, and a buzzy sounding effect dubbed "fuzz." Before long, these devices - along with cabinet-sized tape recorders used to exaggerated whisking and warbling effect - would all shrink in size as vacuum tubes gave way to transistors, and transistors were replaced by microchips. The guitar effects device was now called a "pedal" or "stompbox," and these tiny enclosures were all strung together like a wayward model railroad running across the stage.

While guitar effects acquired a vast and newly experimental tonal vocabulary, new vocabularies developed, as well, in the naming and visual branding of pedals, often exploiting symbols from the culture at large. The stompbox ushered in a whole new and rather specific set of design conventions for form factor, user interface and graphic treatment, which in turn established a utilitarian paradigm with vast possibilities for producing brand identity and bold iconography. The expressive potential was not lost on pedal manufacturers whose thematic forays into popular culture, politics, religion, sexuality, and the cultural conventions of rock 'n' roll unearthed a limitless supply of cultural references for branding and marketing products.

This exhibition also shines a light on some of the mom-and-pop effects houses whose idiosyncratic sensibilities, artistic flair and technical prowess provide ever increasing variety to stompboxes destined for a wide global market. Finally, "PedalCulture" offers a glimpse into the community of Praise & Worship liturgical musicians and pedal users whose lofty aspirations result in different (and often conflicting) sets of attitudes about a working guitarist's pedals of choice and prohibitions.

Introduction

Surf 'n' Turf

pedal

4

culture

Icons of Allusion and Authenticity

The issue of "authenticity" is pervasive throughout the entire world of stompbox musical effects irrespective of effects type. And there is a world of reason for this as guitar effects pedals are rarely self-referential; mostly they refer to something else. At their most basic, effects pedals are designed to produce a tonal effect that recognizably fits into a known family of effects. The tonal reference might be spoken of in a general way ("delay"), or refer to a particular kind of technology ("tape delay"), or perhaps to a unique brand-identified effect (Roland Space Echo delay). Reaching beyond a basic functional reference, the design or naming of a stompbox often evokes something more abstract as it subtly channels an idea, a value, an image or a cultural theme from the larger world courted by the device. Alternately, an effects pedal might employ a stiff outstretched arm pointing at a prominent external reference and sticking a finger in the eye of the original. As the philosopher Thomas Hobbs wryly observed, life is brutish.

The victim of said assault is one Bill Finnegan who, some 25 years ago, had the good fortune to create one of the most vaunted effects pedals ever, the Klon Centaur, thus resulting in its becoming one of the most copied. Hand-built by Finnegan one at a time, the Centaur was a pretty rare beast from the get-go; and, due to a number of factors limiting the amount of production (one being that Bill sold only to people who passed a telephone interview), there was more than ample reason for this pedal to be cloned by others. Aside from its rarity, the Centaur enjoys legendary status (some might call it "mythic") due to its claim as the first overdrive (mild distortion) pedal not to unduly color guitar tone, and also because Finnegan chose to goop up the works in each pedal in black epoxy so as to prevent successful spying. Nevertheless, the market is flooded with purported Klon copies ("klones"), and the number of manufacturers and small builders releasing their own take on the Centaur only continues to grow. To see how these Klon-a-likes are branded with suggestive names, graphics, color schemes, and form factors echoing the original is a fascinating exercise in the importance of symbols, the power of allusion and the problem of authenticity.

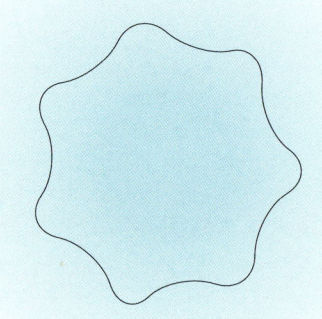

Nowhere is the musical analogy to the natural world more obvious than in surf music (with apologies to Debussy), where staccato guitar and drumbeats drive home the image of crashing surf and the splendor and bravado of riding big waves. In the world of guitar effects, reverb has a place all its own due to a close association between the effect and its common use in early '60s surf music (although, as is often the case with nostalgia, reverb was not nearly so pervasive among early surf bands as it is currently in retro-surf music). So closely are reverb and surf music aligned that one type, spring reverb, has a quality often described as "surfy" or "wet."

For many, it's difficult to hear a spring reverb laden guitar riff without thinking, perhaps longingly, of the beach. In the heyday of surf music, guitarists relied on large enclosed spring reverb tanks and, later on, on smaller tanks found inside Fender amplifiers. While not actual spring reverbs, small-format stompboxes approximating the "boing" of spring reverb are now found everywhere, and designs often evoke the surfing lifestyle in the product's name or graphic treatment of the pedal enclosure. But the most iconic symbol is probably the spring itself, and that, too, can be a whimsical piece of iconography alluding to the authenticity of what's found inside - even though digital processors now stand in for actual springs. In live performance, original model Fender reverb tanks still reign supreme. This fact has not been lost on stompbox designers who employ a somewhat more hardcore approach with appropriate typographic script, color, layout, and control knob style evoking a visual simulacrum of an iconic 1960s reverb tank. Street cred be damned: As they say in the fashion industry, image is everything.

🌸 FRV-1 '63 Fender Reverb

Boss
2009
Japan
Toto guitarist Steve Lukather
  original signature on pedal enclosure
Loan courtesy of Roland Corporation

🌸 FDR-1 '65 Deluxe Reverb

Boss
2015
Japan
Loan courtesy of Pedal Genie

🌸 Spring Theory

SubDecay
2012
USA
Design: Brian Marshall
Curator's private collection

🌸 Boing Spring Reverb

J. Rockett Audio Designs
2017
USA
Loan courtesy of Pedal Genie

🟦 Spring King Reverb

Danelectro
2016
USA
Loan courtesy of Ryan Burke

🟦 Topanga

Catalinbread Mechanisms of Music
2017
USA
Design: Howard Gee, Nicholas Harris,
   Boris Lutskovsky
Artist: David Medel
Loan courtesy of Catalinbread
   Mechanisms of Music

🟢 Centaur

Klon
1996
USA
Design: Bill Finnegan
Numbered 309
Loan courtesy of Joe Gore

🟢 Klon Klone

(generic product)
2017
China
Loan courtesy of Real Guitars

pedal — Surf 'n' Turf: Icons of Allusion and Authenticity — culture

⬡ Tumnus

Wampler Pedals
2017
USA
Design: Brian Wampler
Loan courtesy of Wampler Pedals

⬢ Archer Ikon

J. Rockett Audio Designs
2017
USA
Loan courtesy of Pedal Genie

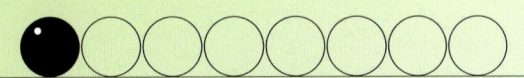

Artisanal Pedal Creations

pedal culture

The business of guitar effects is often associated with highly recognizable and well established brands such as Boss, Electro-Harmonix, DigiTech, TC Electronic and a few others, while music insiders will recognize manufacturing newcomers Donner, Joyo, Mooer and countless other inexpensive Chinese brands filling the market - but in truth, this is an industry of small-time tinkerers. To this day, most effects pedal designs originate on basement workbenches, in backwoods sheds or on someone's dining room table, and many pedals are finished there, too, wired and hand-soldered one piece at a time. "Boutique" pedals, as they're known, are becoming the industry's new norm as hobbyist-tinkerers christen ateliers where all the technical know-how, design, artwork and production is in-house, with pedals assembled by one set of hands, start to finish.

In these makeshift environments, design inspiration, technical wizardry and production standards vary widely from one builder to another. Some builders put sonic originality above all else and direct their focus to the inner workings, courting the most elite rockers as customers. Other builders are content to make small modifications to already popular circuits and look for market inroads with unique branding and clever marketing. Some builders create fantastical artwork, novel identities and outlandish backstory where others are content to use a generic looking box. Despite these differences, boutique builders around the globe are known for originality in design and personal expressiveness; for pride in workmanship and sourcing quality parts and construction; and for diving headlong into hard work, serving up good value as public commodity.

This exhibit brings together a rich harvest of artisanal pedal design. As you look at this and the other displays, you'll see plenty of examples of small-batch pedals - from the humble household of newlyweds to the forge of an injured horseshoer, from the hamlet of an unemployed journalist to the lab of a research scientist. And one domestic operation where the crop of pedals is literally farm to table.

Joe Gore is a local treasure. Look him up. Just for starters, Joe's guitar playing has graced the records of Tom Waits, PJ Harvey and Tracy Chapman, and his YouTube guitar and effects demos are as witty and charming as the genre allows. A consummate musician, Joe is also a tinkerer's tinkerer with great technical design chops, making his small line of effects pedals as praiseworthy as fine wine. Joe routinely tears down guitars and amps to the chassis and modifies and rebuilds them to his own diabolical specs (check out the Hello Kitty Strat with built-in fuzz effect for one ferocious sounding cat!).

The Joe Gore Duh Remedial Fuzz was created in San Francisco (natch!) and is built in Michigan by skilled craftspeople earning a fair wage. The instructions read: "How to use: Turn the knob to make it louder. Duh." Joe must be master of the understatement, as this pedal does it all. Just like Joe himself.

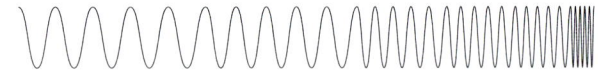

Duh Remedial Fuzz

Joe Gore
2017
USA
Loan courtesy of Joe Gore

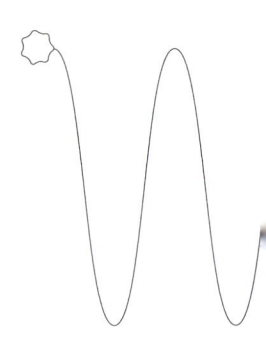

Visiting the Spruce Effects Web site is a visceral experience, much like in the once unavoidable Irish Spring TV commercial where you're welcomed to the vibrancy of nature with eyes, ears and nose. As a bar of soap might transport you to the green and pristine, so it is with the Spruce Old Growth Fuzz. Scrolling past photos of mountains and meadows, sprigs and springs, you find the pedal itself, an illustration on its housing decorated with the beautiful grain of a plank of wood, and at once you smell the pine forest. "Inspired by variations of the classic muff," the text reads, "and the haunting and sustaining old growth Spruce forests of Norway, this fuzz is dynamic, heavy, and in your face."

"Made with love in California. Spruce Effects is a small, one man, one woman outfit in the greater Bay Area of California. Every pedal is made by the two of us, and all our pedals are beautiful and well-made. We custom design, hand-build, and love all of our effects equally. Every pedal is painstakingly designed and crafted in-house. Our goal is to create classic sounds in a custom, modern package that can be used for any situation."

Value and virtue, Spruce Effects pedals are heartfelt like family, real as hand-hewn and true as nature itself.

Old Growth Fuzz

Spruce Effects
2017
USA
Design: Brian Bicknell
Loan courtesy of Spruce Effects

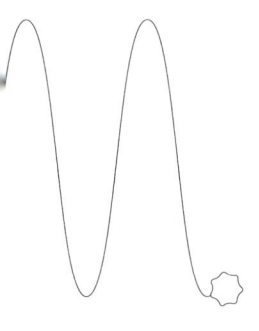

Everything Geof Hancock and his family do is homegrown. In the summer they run Hancock Family Farm in Casco, Maine, growing vegetables organically for the local co-op and farmers' market. And in the winter, Geof builds over a hundred effects pedals by hand while his wife makes guitar straps. The family economy depends on their selling guitar accessories and channeling profit back into the farm fueling their primary source of work. As Geof puts it, "When you run a farm, all money is farm money."

From the mouth of Geof: "The pedal market is a big pie, so there are a lot of slices to go around. Innovation isn't even always what people are looking for. They want something personal and honest, familiar but with its own flavor. I'm the only one building Farm Pedals right now, all by hand. I have a lot of flexibility. I can change things on the fly. And if it fails, it's not going to be the end of me."

Geof sent over one of his organic, farm fresh pedals for display in a table exhibit. It's called the High Pass Boost, and it's the color of wheat straw. You know what they sometimes say: It's so good, it ought to be illegal.

High Pass Boost

Farm Pedals
2017
USA
Design: Geof Hancock
Loan courtesy of Farm Pedals

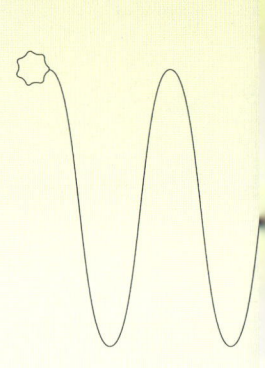

Artisanal Pedal Creations

Ed Chew's pedals convey the distinct look of handcrafted forged steel, produced in his shop in Prairie Farm, Wisconsin. Ed's no stranger to anvils, fire and forging, an injury having made him lay down the hammer and tongs of his trade as a farrier (def: one who trims and shoes horses' hooves) for the intricacies of guitar pedal design. Luckily, he says, "custom shaping hot steel to the shape of individual horses' feet has helped me develop a style of working that transfers over into electronic design very nicely, a combination of art and science." DIY beginnings led to a successful Kickstarter campaign funding his line of effects pedals.

The Orcrist Overdrive is named after the sword in J.R.R. Tolkien's novel, *The Hobbit*. Made by the Elven smiths of Middle Earth, Orcrist had a beautiful scabbard and jeweled hilt; there were runes on the sword which bore its name, and it took on a blue glow when enemy Orcs were near. Referencing the legendary sword in Tolkien's story, the pedal itself features the name Orcrist in Gondolin runes cut out and back-lit with blue LED's when the pedal is switched on. By all outward appearances, the Orcrist Overdrive shows as a beautiful relic of Middle Earth.

Orcist Overdrive

Wrought Iron Leather and Effects
2017
USA
Design: Ed Chew
Loan courtesy of Wrought Iron Leather and Effects

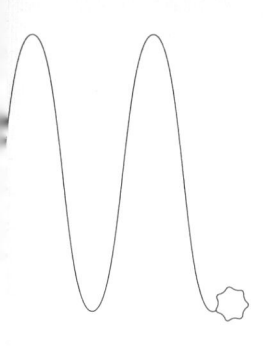

Mark Svirkov's SviSound is recognized for great sounding, technically innovative pedal designs that find their home in distinctive steampunk and grunge metal styled enclosures.

Mark got his start in guitar effects in 1978 when he got the wild notion to construct an effects pedal for use in his school band. This was in Russia, where in 1988 he opened his first company before moving to Bulgaria in 2013. Mark has four workers who assist him in hand-wiring circuits and building original enclosures. SviSound stompboxes easily convey a Jules Verne fin de siècle retro-futuristic appeal with Victorian styled features and cases made of drilled, milled, engraved and galvanized raw metal.

About his creations, Mark says: "I'm building pedals with original sounds, I never make copies from other manufacturers. My components are really unique and the circuit design is a result of much experimentation. I also use a lot of time to create unique enclosures. Often it is longer than the soldering and adjustment. But my buyers get unique devices with unique sounds in unique cases."

🟡 EchoZoid

SviSound
2017
Bulgaria
Design: Mark Svirkov
Loan courtesy of SviSound

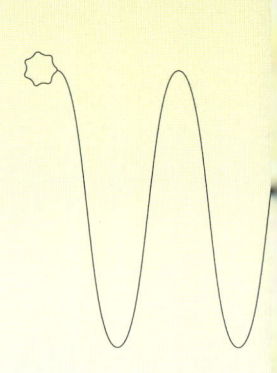

With names like GUNSHOT, FALLOUT CLOUD, and PEACEKEEPER you're probably not surprised to learn ThorpyFX founder Adrian Thorpe is a retired major in the British Army. ThorpyFX is his post-career, career. ThorpyFX pedals have a cold, calculated, steely look that make them stand out as objects of sharp high-tech industrial design, distinguishing them from more common and homier boutique crafted devices. The WARTHOG exhibits a peace sign laser etched into a stainless steel enclosure offering an unlikely reference to its namesake, the A-10 Thunderbolt fighter aircraft used by the U. S. in Iraq and Afghanistan. If you happen to be born in the year of the warthog (does one even exist?) your signature virtues are: Ability to sense danger, courage, protection, and the ability to find the truth. This distortion pedal has a lot to live up to.

ThorpyFX is a family run business located in Wiltshire, England. The team is made up of Adrian, his wife Georgia, and Oppenheimer the dog.

The WARTHOG Distortion

ThorpyFX
2017
England
Loan courtesy of Pedal Genie

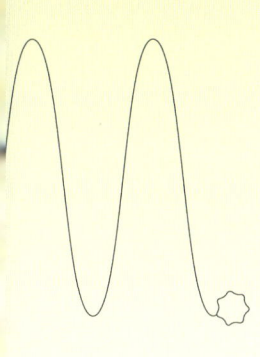

Back in the days before "reuse" took on an arty cachet, the OctaHive would have been referred to as "junkyard chic," a term consisting of somewhat equal parts praise and damnation. Of course, now we all know the importance of diverting consumer waste from landfill and finding other uses for the discarded and disregarded. And, we've learned to show the world how nifty and thrifty we can be with our hands. Clearly, times have changed – and practical, ethical and artful are today's principles of production. Welcome the Beetronics Custom series of individually designed and crafted effects pedals, where each object is an original work of art. True to de Saint-Exupéry's endearing sentiment, each Beetronics pedal is "unique in all the world."

Beetronics says "We are a family business formed by a guitar player, a drummer, a journalist, an architect and a dog. Our pedals are handmade in California. Every pedal we make is unique, hand made and there are no two exactly alike. We have fun while doing it."

OctaHive

Beetronics
2017
USA
Loan courtesy of Beetronics

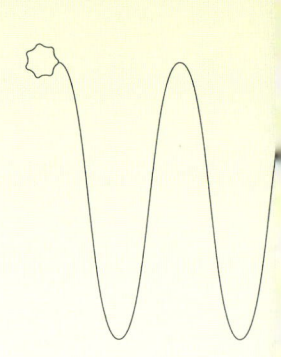

Artisanal Pedal Creations

If outward appearance means anything, then the utterly novel creations exiting the workshop of Dr. No earn him the distinction of the "Dr. Frankenstein" of the guitar effects world. At its most harmless, visiting the Eindhoven laboratory of Dr. No in the Netherlands might be as we imagine a visit to Doc Brown's lab in *Back to the Future*. An avuncular presence, maybe; zany, for sure. The pedals themselves? Totally wacky, with grotesque decorative doodads derived from sci-fi, horror and fantasy; and then some cheerful cartoon-like imagery employed in the design of this, the Road Runner Flying Wah. Unlike other devices in this display, Dr. No pedals are not from the city and not from the farm, but they come from the land of make-believe.

This design was made for and in collaboration with David Catching, guitarist and owner of the famed Rancho De La Luna recording studio in Joshua Tree. Befitting the odd oeuvre of Dr. No it's no surprise that the Flying Machina comes with a warning: "This device actually flies!!! Dr. No and Dave can not be held responsible for any physical damage like broken bones, just because you can't fly the damn thing..."

Road Runner Octave FuzzWah Flying Machina

Dr. No Effects
2017
Netherlands
Design: Dr. No, David Catching
Loan courtesy of Dr. No Effects

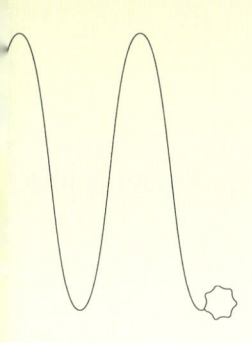

🟡 Troy Van Leeuwen "TVL" Octavia

Dr. No Effects
2017
Netherlands
Design: Dr. No
Numbered #50/100
Loan courtesy of Dr. No Effects

With the Roadrunner and Holy Wahcamole wah pedals Dr. No shows an extraordinarily vivacious and playful personality at work - "at play?" But with the TVL Octavia, designed in collaboration with guitarist Troy van Leeuwen, Dr. No's visual aesthetics go darker and the effects rock especially hard. Employed on the recently released Queens of the Stone Age record "Villains," the guitar effect was called "carnivalesque, disco inferno, and devil-may-care experimentation all wrapped up into one" - an apt characterization of the "TVL" pedal design itself.

The Alain Johannes 11:11 auto wah/fuzz is a bird of a different feather, having been designed and developed in collaboration with rock guitarist Alain Johannes, co-founder of the group Eleven. The 11:11 is perhaps best understood as a personal Ouija board of symbolic associations and evocations drawn from the details of Johannes' life and relationships. Designed to reflect matrimonial ideals of harmony and cooperation, rotating the chicken skulls (stand-ins for Alain and his deceased wife) causes your guitar tone to go from balanced to chaotic, throwing your musical future to the winds of fate.

In matters concerning himself, Dr. No speaks reticently. He allows only this much: "My name is Dr. No. I make Art for musicians and artists to inspire them to create Music and Art. I collaborate with Musicians and Artists that inspire me to bring you the world's finest musical gear experience, capture their DNA and put this into functional Art for you to purchase and use. I do not create for commercial businesses, musical instruments industry and or shops, but only for people that are passionate about Art and Music. Every single creation is built with passion and created by me and only me."

Alain Johannes 11:11

Dr. No Effects
2015
Netherlands
Design: Dr. No
Numbered #121/121
Loan courtesy of Dr. No Effects

Pedaling Popular Culture

🟠 Dr FREAKENSTEIN FUZZ DRFF-3LE

Rainger FX
2009
England
Design: David Rainger
Art: Rich DiMaio
Limited production run of 30
Pedal comes with "Igor" foot controller
Loan courtesy of Rainger FX

As relevant a discourse for our current age as ever before, Mary Shelly's 1818 novel, *Frankenstein* - brought to life in the original movie adaptation of 1931 - exploits anxieties over our love-hate relationship with modern technology and the inevitable queasiness around whom (or what) we'll wake up with in the morning. Aside from big literary questions of life and death, spirit and matter, and existential insecurity over the future of humanity itself, *Frankenstein* (the movie) is vividly recalled as a highly theatrical, dark extravaganza of great visual tropes drawn from retro sci-fi Machine Age depictions of technology. The Dr FREAKENSTEIN FUZZ is just one more in an endless string of goofs, spoofs and Catskills-style schtick on the Frankenstein motif, and aren't we glad it is. From all accounts - musical and otherwise - this is one monster of a pedal! So, get your freak on.

Kongpressor

Kong needs no introduction; in fact, he often gets the last word. In the case of the Kongpressor, the pun isn't lost on guitarists looking to squish the volume extremes of their guitar under force of insurmountable compression. Special recognition goes to scene stealer Fay Wray, with honorable mention to Big Ben and the River Thames.

Charlie Fuzz

Charles Manson is a complicated subject, and any commentary on the Charlie Fuzz pedal is subject to endless complications, as well. Perhaps this pedal serves as a Rorschach for a viewer's feelings about Manson the incarcerated serial killer, or for his shapeshifting persona in popular culture. Whatever else, this stompbox will be a canvas for controversy. Australia's Kink Guitar Pedals plays

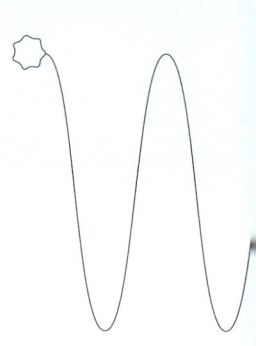

Kongpressor

Orange Pedals
2017
England
Loan courtesy of Orange USA

Pedaling Popular Culture

26

it close to the vest, saying their pedals are "Not safe for children. You will not find any cute pedal artwork here." (Is this meant as a social disclaimer?) Manson's anti-hero status in the popular culture looms large, a notorious black hat for half a century. The Manson legacy enjoys a position as a niche media specimen, and from prison Manson welcomed the attention of a devoted and, for some, adoring cadre of followers. Given the mythology surrounding "Helter Skelter" (Manson's violent call to revolution), we might wonder whether the Charlie Fuzz lands as a perverse icon of social alienation, crashing through the din of frustration for people willing to tear down institutions - to "blow things up" - regardless the consequences? Or is the Charlie Fuzz merely an apt metaphor for a wild and unpredictable fuzz effect with a penchant for acting real crazy? Plug it in, and the eyes light up. Charlie's gaze is upon you.

Charlie Fuzz

Kink Guitar Pedals
2017
Australia
Design: Mark Quarrell
Numbered #09
Curator's private collection

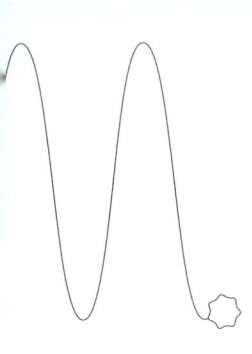

The guitar world loves fuzz. Where other effects seek light, fuzz is dark, dangerous and destructive. Fuzz drives to the extreme. Fuzz dares you to want more. Fuzz takes no prisoners. Fuzz takes you straight to hell, so say Wren and Cuff, with the release of the Irkalla Manifest Fuzz pedal. Irkalla is the underworld destination where, as described on Sumerian and Babylonian roadmaps of the time, souls of the dead dwelled for eternity. It's also a nifty planet in the vast Star Wars mythology of the Lucas constellation. That's Irkalla's ruler, the goddess Ereshkigal, depicted by artist Tony Coppin as the gatekeeper no mortal could love.

Irkalla Manifest Fuzz

Wren and Cuff
2017
USA
Art: Tony Coppin
Loan courtesy Wren and Cuff

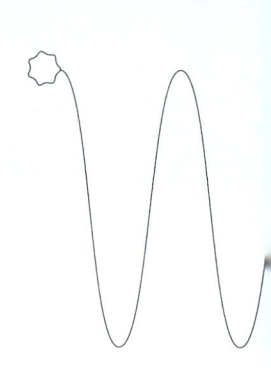

For most builders it would be enough to add a 20 db signal boost, jolting the amp from its slumber and taunting it into frenzied overdrive. But London's TateFX has something else up its sleeve, requiring we put on our high waders for a trek through the muck of contemporary American politics. Just when you thought it could get no deeper, the device boosts the BS, rubbing our noses in the stench of the bully pulpit while delivering just the boost a guitarist needs to cut through the crap. TateFX hit its stride with the Brexit Means Brexit maximum distortion pedal with controls for "racism" and "recession," but why dip into someone else's fear and loathing when foul waters are rising so much closer to home.

Bullshit Booster

TateFX
2017
England
Design: Stuart Tate
Numbered #11
Curator's private collection

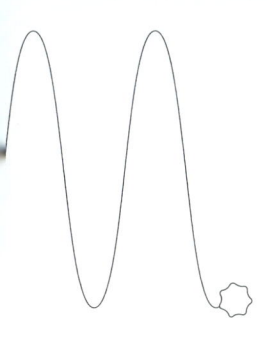

The Greenhouse Effects "27 Club" series of pedals takes quite a hit for being morbid. But then, rock isn't for the squeamish, is it? Rock rocks the boat and rocks it hard. The club in question, for those not so initiated, is the growing list of rockers dead at 27. Greenhouse Effects illustrations pull no punches with graphic depictions of the cause (if not the actual moment) of death. While a small adjustment to name or image might put a more sentimental spin on the subject, clearly such was not the intent with "27 Club." These pedals are brash and more than a little brutal, and they induce an attitude adjustment for anyone who thinks they might get out of here alive.

Roadkiller

Greenhouse Effects
2017
Israel
Numbered #192
Curator's private collection

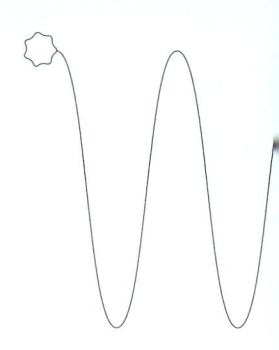

How do you brand a savage pedal geared for maximum distortion of modern metal? You go black. And if it doesn't refer to real-life murder and arson (Abominable Electronics' Throne Torcher, exhibited in A Pedal for Your Thoughts) you name it after make-believe murder and arson. That would be "dracarys" (dragonfire), the command given to loyal dragons prompting their action in the lethal roasting of one's enemies, the incineration of ships and the light grilling of meats, in TV's popular "Game of Thrones" (drawn from a series of fantasy novels by George R. R. Martin). "Dracarys" comes from the fictitious High Valyrian language, and has nicely made its way into our own pop culture lexicon as a sort of modern-day "fie upon thee," only with a lot more singe.

The Dracarys

Wampler Pedals
2017
USA
Design: Brian Wampler
Loan courtesy of Wampler Pedals

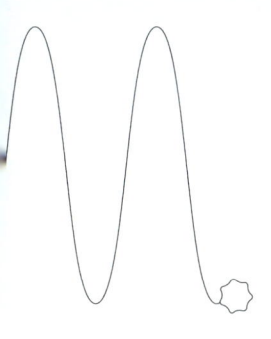

Hatsune Miku is a virtual pop culture sensation. She looks very much like a 16-year-old girl with long turquoise "twintails," but her apparent material reality is actually the glossy veneer of a computer generated character brought to you by Krypton Future Media. Miku's singing voice is sampled from Japanese voice actress Saki Fujita, making Hatsune Miku a big on-stage hit as an animated projection hologram at Fujita's performances. There is always something new for Miku to perform as she is reputed to have a catalog of over 100,000 unique songs to her name. Her American debut on "The Late Show with David Letterman" stunned audiences who fondly recalled other foreigners with odd-looking hairdos performing on that very same stage some 50 years earlier.

Korg's Miku Stomp is a handsome pedal and a fitting tribute to one of Japan's biggest stars (the "Immaterial Girl"?), and so much the better if the effect's sole purpose is to turn people's guitars into hosts for Hatsune Miku's synthesized vocal talents. The pedal is capable of playing Japanese phrases in pitch with the guitar, or can be primed to spit out Japanese sounding phonetics and nonsense syllables. Within the rather large world of YouTube guitar gear fandom the Miku Stomp has become a pop culture phenomenon in its own right.

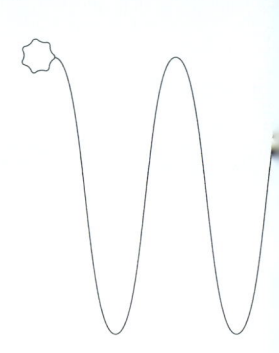

🟠 Miku Stomp

Korg
2014-15
Japan
Curator's private collection

In the slightly wacky world of Idiot-Box Effects you can buy a Death Ray Frequency Mangler or peruse kitschy and colorful movie graphics of Jeff Spicoli, *Young Frankenstein* and Hans Solo fronting pedal enclosures. Another effect, named after a beloved TV character (played by Nick Offerman of "Parks and Recreation"), is the Ron Fucking Swanson Superfuzz. The humor is ironic and dry to the bone.

IdiotBox Effects is Atarimatt. Atarimatt may or may not be Christopher M. Shea of College Station, Texas, who was kind enough to send along this pedal. We suspect he may have written the following (actual, but edited for brevity) Wikipedia entry for College Station: "In the 1990s, College Station and Texas A&M University drew national attention when the George Bush Presidential Library opened in 1997 and, more tragically, when 12 people were killed and 27 injured when the Aggie Bonfire collapsed while being constructed in 1999. Bobby Jaramillo from Huntsville, TX once claimed College Station was a metropolitan utopia. However, thru reliable sources such as Forbes, College Station proved to be another small hick town in East Texas. College Station failed to rank as one of the fastest growing cities and for some delusional reason people located in and near Houston inaccurately claim this small town is otherworldly." Product and place, cut from the same cloth.

Ron Fucking Swanson Fuzz

IdiotBox Effects
2017
USA
Loan courtesy of IdiotBox Effects

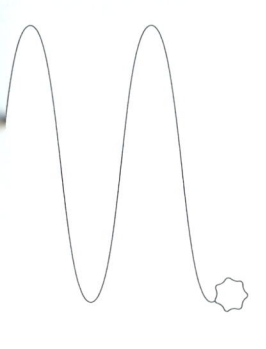

Holy Wahcamoly

pedal culture

34

culture

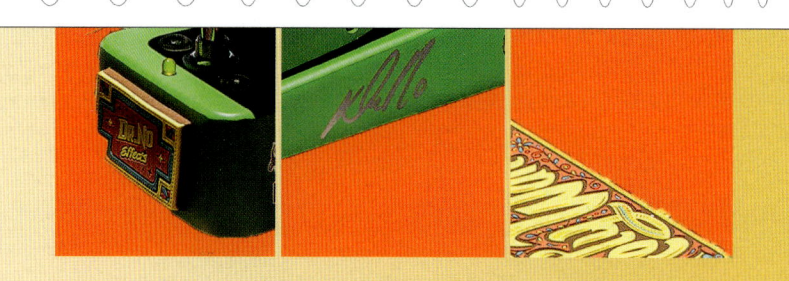

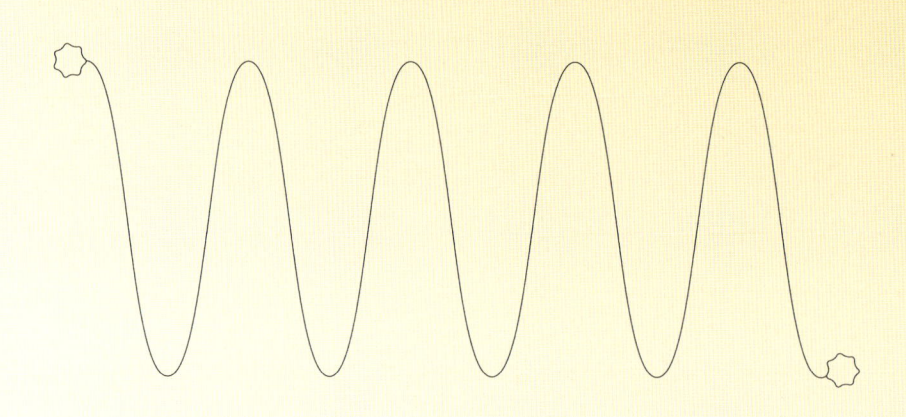

pedal Holy Wahcamoly culture
36

🟢 Holy Wahcamoly

Dr. No Effects
2017
Netherlands
Design: Dr. No
Art: Eric van den Boom
Signed by Dr. No
Loan courtesy of Dr. No Effects
Favors courtesy of Casa Sanchez SF
Effects pedal, decorative display & complimentary tortilla chip dispensary

How did he ever get that sound? From the early days of effects pedals and the iconic buzz of Keith Richards' Maestro Fuzz-Tone in "Satisfaction" (1965) we were startled by sounds we'd never before heard, and we stirred to a whole new *sonic lexicon*

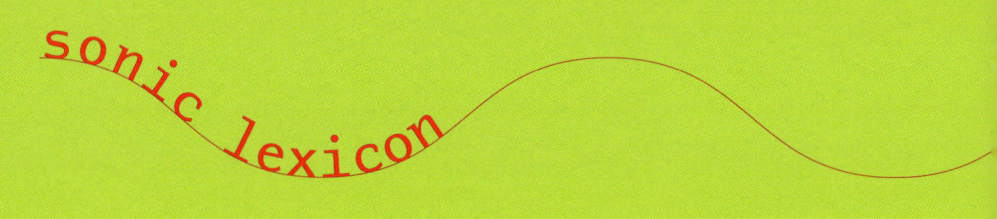

Rock It 8/8

The advent of the effects stompbox allowed many popular songs their signature guitar tone as the songs in Rock It 8/8 bear testament. But beyond the sonic is the symbolic. Pedals can be weighty symbols, and like any object of power they have the authority to convey the mojo of past association to any would-be believer who comes in contact. The effects pedals you hear in Rock It 8/8 have become true fetish objects. Their electrical components convey near mystical properties bridging a budding guitarist's humble strumming to the guitar solos of legendary performances and bygone performers. Rabid tone hunters and serious devotees of these musical performances will want to own the exact model pedal used on the recording. As clothes make the man, the tones make the musician – and these pedals are dressed for success. Pay close attention to the sounds you hear...then turn on, plug in, and tune down.

ANDREW STOCKDALE
Song: Joker and the Thief
Pedal used: Micro Synth
Manufacturer: EHX

pedal   Rock it 8/8   cultur
                            40

Jerry Garcia
"Fire on the Mountain"
Musitronics Mu-Tron III
envelope filter

Kurt Cobain
"Come as You Are"
Electro-Harmonix Small Clone
chorus

Keith Richards
"(I Can't Get No) Satisfaction"
Maestro FZ-1 Fuzz-tone
fuzz

Charles "Skip" Pitt
"Theme from Shaft"
Maestro Boomerang
wah

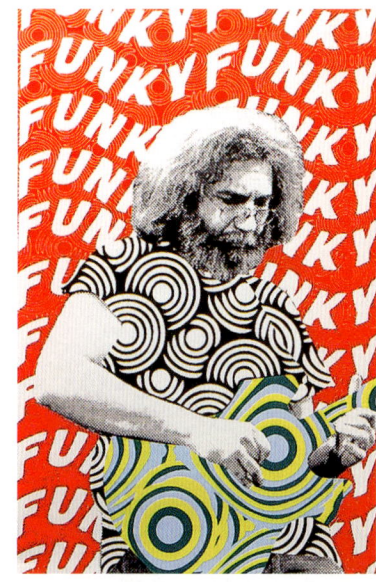

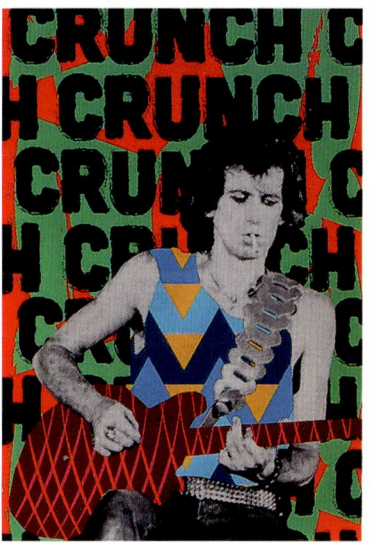

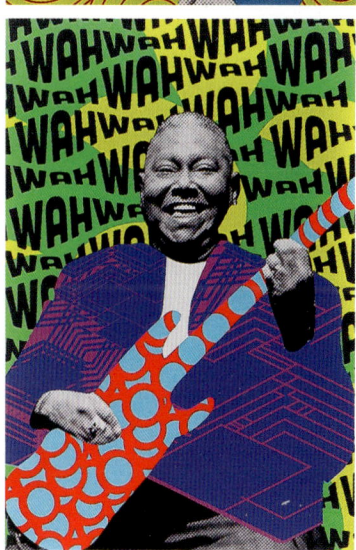

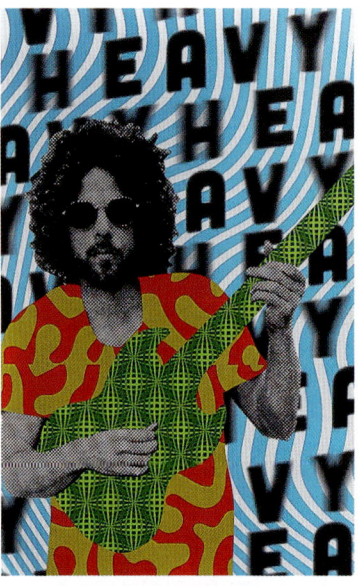

David Gilmour

"Comfortably Numb"
Electro-Harmonix Big Muff Pi
(Ram's Head version)
fuzz

Andrew Stockdale

"Joker & the Thief"
Electro-Harmonix Microsynth
analog synthesizer

The Edge

"Pride (In the Name of Love)"
Electro-Harmonix Deluxe Memory Man
analog delay

Jimi Hendrix

"Machine Gun"
Univox Uni-Vibe
uni-vibe

pedal culture

43

The Mosrite Fuzzrite is one of several popular fuzz pedals of the 1960s. While each type of fuzz effect has its devoted following, the Fuzzrite holds a special place in the

palpitating hearts and freaked out minds

of '60s music aficionados. The effect's full-on raspy buzz was famously employed by heavy psychedelic music makers Iron Butterfly and by a host of local San Francisco bands. Fuzzrite also was the fuzz of choice for peppering sonic aggression and raunch into exploitation movie soundtracks of the era and added audio excitation to the first blush of mainstream porn.

Mosrite   Fuzzrite

The Mosrite Fuzzrite is one of several popular fuzz pedals of the 1960s. While each type of fuzz effect has its devoted following, the Fuzzrite holds a special place in the palpitating hearts and freaked out minds of '60s music aficionados. The effect's full-on raspy buzz was famously employed by heavy psychedelic music makers Iron Butterfly, and by a host of local San Francisco bands. Fuzzrite also was the fuzz of choice for peppering sonic aggression and raunch into exploitation movie soundtracks of the era, and for adding audio embellishment to the first blush of mainstream porn.

Movie *Satan's Sadists* (1969)

Music Compilation of biker movie soundtrack music by Davie Allan & the Arrows (1966-67):

Blue's Theme
Devil's Angels
Cody's Theme
The Devil's Rumble
The Young World
Cycle-Delic
Another Cycle in Detroit
Lulu's World
The Stompers and the Souls

Mosrite Fuzzrite

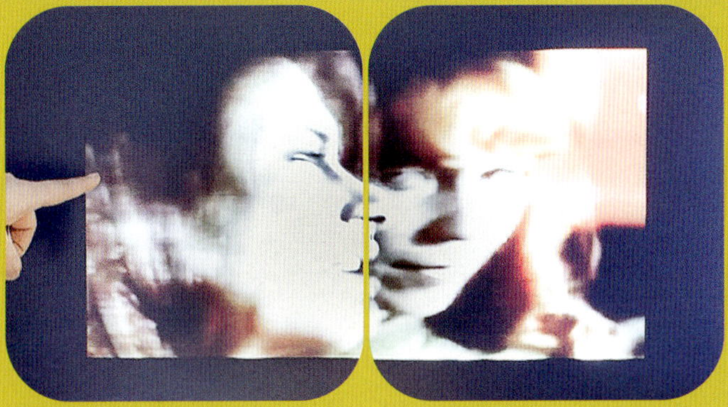

"Does God want the best gear...

or does he want the best care, love and energy spent on the naked, hungry and homeless?"

Heavenly Pedals

The Praise and Worship (PW) music community is a genuine subculture within popular music. In terms of musical style, the music of PW is often indistinguishable from certain styles of commercial pop, but the reasons behind PW performance are fundamentally different from those of secular music. Most importantly, the social, ethical and religious values underlying PW bear little resemblance to many of the prevailing cultural norms in popular music. We can see these distinctions in the respectful attitudes of Christian worship leaders - those guitarists who scrupulously hone to religious principle and purpose - who lead their congregations in musical praise of god. However defined the purpose of PW music may be, as in much of life the reality is never quite that simple. PW guitarists invariably navigate a varied terrain of musical and cultural influences, and must bridge varying religious, secular, artistic and personal impulses often in the course of a single performance. In playing music meant to praise (god) and uplift (the congregation), it's not unusual for the performing guitarist to feel creatively stifled by a repertoire of limited variety and restricted by the conservative attitudes of the congregation. What's more, for PW guitarists the personal choices governing selection and use of musical equipment are subject to a great variety of unresolved ethical issues that would feel totally alien (if not downright absurd) to the secular musician.

Many church guitarists have elaborate pedalboards, many have massively-sized pedalboards, and many of these pedalboards are quite costly. For the secular guitarist, such a display of pedals can be a thing of pride, and certainly a thing of pleasure. And if you happen to be a natural showoff, then this is just one more opportunity to produce envy in the hearts of others. But for the church guitarist, the fact of a showy pedalboard, or an expensive one, is just one more opportunity to feel conflicted about how ego attachment often runs up against more humble and self-effacing virtues more consistent with devoting oneself to the elevation of god.

The following dialogue is drawn from participant-observation studies in a 15,000 member PW online discussion community devoted to guitar gear.

● **Reverb.com music marketplace**

From ambient pads to complex rhythmic synth-sounding lead melodies, the gear a worship guitarist chooses is vital to being able to nail the techniques and tones now required for the genre. And while their pedalboards may look like Mission Control, each of those pedals, amps and guitars play a vital role in delivering the player's message. Boutique quality is paramount.

Timothy Does anyone ever feel like we are missing the point in "bringing our best" to God? Does God want the best gear, riffs and tone, or does he want the best care, love and energy spent on the naked, hungry, homeless and in-prisoned?

Jeremy How can a person of faith seemingly boast or envelop themselves with such extravagance if they are to be the meek, futile, and humble souls that they are called to be? For myself, at least, I do not gloat because I have "nice" gear; I am not boastful. That would be defeating the purpose of what the Gospel is about. For me, it's honestly about passion, devotion, dedication, and service. This board that some presume as an idol, is more of a tool that is used for the glory of my God. The music is worship, and my sole purpose in my ministry is to use it as a conduit to channel God's message to all to the very best of my ability.

David I've brought close to $5,000 worth of my own gear into church services. Jesus is a mighty king and deserves way more than I could ever give, anyway!

John Jesus doesn't care about your fancy gear.

Jeremy Amen. He wants that heart!

Reverb.com If there is one effect you simply can't do without when playing worship-style guitar, it's delay. In many ways, the rhythmic and textural sounds of delay have shaped the sound of modern worship music more than any other musical inspiration. Techniques such as the rhythmic dotted 8th note delays and textural volume swells were taken right from the U2 book of guitar playing, and have become so common that it's hard to find a modern worship song that doesn't incorporate them [using effects pedals].

Kilgore Everyone is so manicured and vanilla with these obvious pop sensibilities. If there is a god, and it created this world, that god seems to me to have more grit and wry humor than this service might allow. The god I'm thinking of might even reward people who weren't sucked into mindless positivity with a veil of barely repressed sexuality as a marketing tool.

Holly I love when our electric guitarists play ambient [long-delay volume swells] because it makes me feel like Heaven is calling me. The feel it has on a room is breathtaking and heavy (in such a powerfully good way that is!) . . . . I believe He uses it all, times of silence and just awe, and times of whooing, and times of flat out jammin' with some heavy electric and drums and bass. It's all amazing and powerful when the reason and purpose behind it all is there to glorify God and to draw closer to Him. Without that, it's just a bunch of bunk noise. With God's presence and acknowledging Him to lead us and the congregation, now that's substance!

PW guitarists are uneasy about calling what they do in church a "performance." They feel strongly about the need to distinguish music as a form of spiritual leadership from the act of playing guitar solely for entertainment (despite the fact they both might appear the same to an outsider). The key distinction is that performance allows for and even encourages self-glorification, while playing music for the congregation can only be about glorifying god. Both forms use guitars, amplifiers and pedals.

Blake

You will never hear me call musicians in a church "performers," because that word means someone who is drawing attention to themselves. In a bar on a Friday night, you are a performer. In a concert outside of church, you are a performer. When you are in church you are a worship leader. Are you doing the same thing? Technically yes, but I like different terms to differentiate and remind me that I'm not focused on me and my performance. All that is to say: if you have the right heart & motive behind it and God is being praised, what more can you ask for?"

Johnny

The funny thing about music is that it always evokes a spiritual response. The vast majority of musicians say they do it for the audience, for the "music," for the Lord, etc. In the end, we all do this because we enjoy giving what we have to others; music is inherently a mechanism for giving to others.

We might do it for the Lord and, in preparation, spend our time and resources. And when we have worked, and prayed, and practiced, and studied, we take to a stage and we present what we have prepared to a group of people that will enjoy it, will exhibit a spiritual response, and will be entertained.

No matter how hard we strive to make our time on Sundays completely spiritual, there is a temporal, corporeal, material aspect to it. God likes these things; he made them. He delights in our enjoyment of what he has made and I believe he equally enjoys seeing what we do with his raw materials. Crafting wood into a guitar that plays excellently is craftsmanship and worship; learning to play it is education and worship; presenting the talent and instruments together is performance and worship.

It's easy to

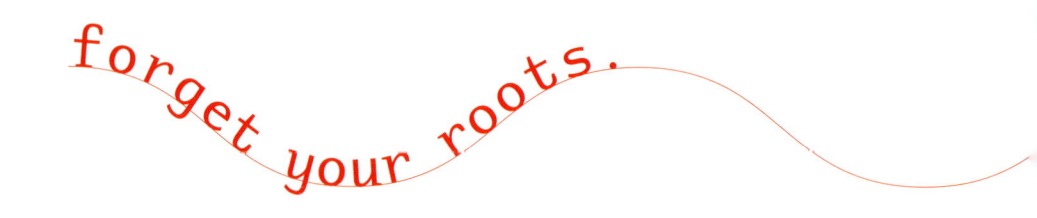

forget your roots.

No matter how technologically advanced they appear to be, many of the effects pedals you see in the display cases around you have

Effects   History

very humble origins in post-War experiments in the mechanics of sound. Rotating speakers, hand-manipulated tape spools, punctured speaker cones, and microphones placed in tiled bathrooms - or in big, outdoor cisterns - all attest to simple but effective ways an audio engineer might enhance or distort the acoustics of recorded sound. While many innovations in recording might well become the stuff of "Popular Mechanics" magazine, other innovations owe their existence to the brilliant (but secretive) genius of guitarist/inventor Les Paul, whose delayed "echo" effects and multi-track tape-recording techniques gave rise to the modern recording studio. This photo display recalls a time before effects pedals when sound was manipulated by hand, in real-time and in real physical space.

1
Reel-to-Reel Audiotape Recorder

In physically manipulating the tape on large reel-to-reel machines operating engineers developed new sonic effects such as flange, and created repeating loops of recorded effects (as made famous by the Beatles on the 1966 song "Tomorrow Never Knows").

2
Watkins Copicat (tape echo)

Tape echo was a popular '50s rock 'n' roll effect created by simultaneous recording and playing back of instruments at different locations on a single loop of tape. The Watkins Copicat was a popular device from England.

3
Roland Space Echo (tape echo)

A more advanced unit than the earlier Watkins Copicat, beginning in the 1970s the Roland Space Echo afforded more control and flexibility in adding engineered effects. Each kind of branded echo device added its own particular color of sonic manipulation to the recording of musical performance.

4
Plate Reverb

A particularly desirable form of studio reverb, plate reverb has a vibrancy well suited to vocals and drums. The device is comprised of a thin sheet of metal suspended within a rigid frame. A transducer vibrates the plate, the sound of which is picked up by a microphone.

5
Spring Reverb Tank

Similar to plate reverb in effect, but much smaller, this device utilizes the reverberations of springs to create a twangy sound most effective for enhancing guitar tone.

6
Leslie Speaker

The Leslie speaker is a combined amplifier and speaker that projects the signal from an electric instrument, modifying the sound with a rotating baffle to create a truly unique warbly, washy musical effect.

7
Echo Chamber

Physical enclosures – everything from a tiled bathroom or long hallway to an outdoor cistern – were employed in the service of reverberating speaker output into a microphone, creating a highly desirable echo effect for guitar, drums and other instruments.

pedal — Effects History — culture

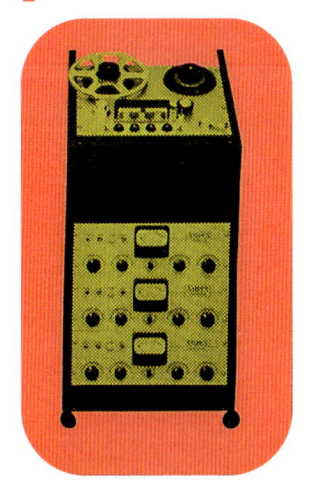

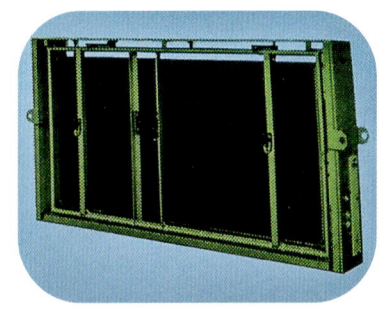

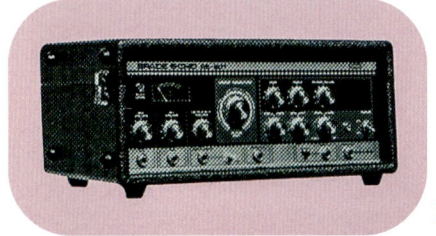

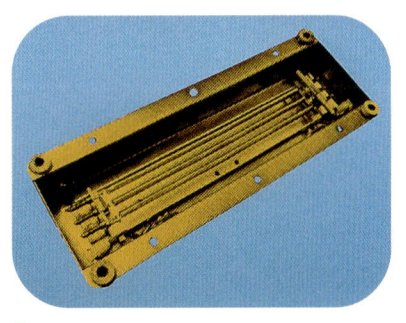

1

4

2

6

3

5

7

57

The Hall of Fame 2 Reverb delivers some of the most iconic reverb sounds

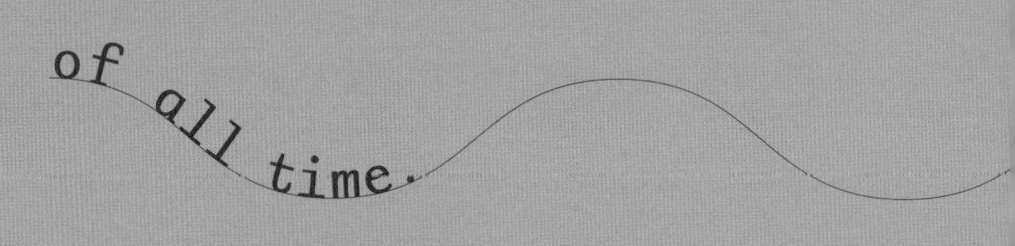

of all time.

Developed by Danish company TC Electronic and employing its proprietary TonePrint computer technology, this pedal offers guitarists custom tailored effects via personal adjustments to all internal settings. Play with the sliders and parameters on the screen to hear alterations to the sound in real-time. And on the pedal itself you physically control external parameters with the MASH function, a switch that reacts to the amount of pressure applied. The harder you press, the more intense the effect. Two physical knobs control the intensity and the sustain of the effect, and everything else is up to your own experimentation using the software provided. Not just for rock stars, the Hall of Fame 2 gives everybody the tools to create their own personally customized reverb. Go ahead, create!

Hall of Fame 2

Tell   Me

pedal   60   culture

a Story

Humanity would be far less human without the capacity for storytelling. In stories passed down as origin and creation myths we learn who we are, where we came from, and the cosmic machinations of how we came into being. As a village elder might trace a people's mythological origins to a natural world teeming with sources for rich cultural connection, we find the chiefs of pedal design looking to the world at large for the semiotics of association and symbolic but superficial connection. A pedal's beginnings might allow as to a cosmic moment of creation going back to deep space, or summon the seminal events inside a nuclear reactor gone kaflooey. We are told of the origins of the Ayahuasca pedal "within the heart of the Amazon jungle," as its "potent psychedelic panacea induces vivid auditory sensations for the musician and listener," likening the device to an exotic drug and cultural practices found in a remote rainforest. While these mythologized narratives serve up a facetiously bastardized "form follows fantasy," other pedal names conjure their own backstories rooted in familiar and not so familiar literary sources from which character and place names, and mood, are appropriated. Here, too, story imprints an identity, connecting the pedal's character as a musical device to an expressive narrative extracted from published poetry or prose. More factual than fanciful are true-life origins (as tantalizing as some reality TV program) in which an effects pedal is named after a "person of interest" or signifies a bonafide historical event through the use of artwork or other design references. To the archaeologist or designer, every artifact has a story to tell. The effects pedals in this exhibit announce their intentions with bold allusions to religious, literary, anecdotal and historical events, and collaterally in artful depictions of original, fantastical settings. You can read them like a book.

On April 19, 1943, a day that would be remembered as "Bicycle Day," the noted Swiss chemist Albert Hofmann dosed himself with LSD-25 in the first in a series of experiments to learn the properties of the pharmaceutical substance he'd successfully synthesized in the laboratory. After a rapid onset of mental instability and hallucinogenic visions, Hoffman knew he had to get home. Due to automobile shortages during the war, he traveled home by bicycle dodging phantom objects as he rode. Once home, Hoffman relaxed into the "kaleidoscopic, fantastic images [that] surged in on me . . . opening and then closing themselves in circles and spirals, exploding in colored fountains, rearranging and hybridizing themselves in constant flux."

Catalinbread effects designer Nicholas Harris christened the Bicycle Delay after the mind-altering experiences reported in Hoffman's personal journal, saying "the Bicycle Delay is a physical manifestation of the experience of consciousness, letting go of the desire to control everything. The more I surrendered to what it was showing me, the more it set me free to be musically creative." With controls for Lucidity, Reflect, Mood and Expanse, the story is within.

Bicycle Delay

Catalinbread Mechanisms of Music
2017
USA
Design: Nicholas Harris, Howard Gee
Art: David Medel
Loan courtesy of Catalinbread Mechanisms of Music

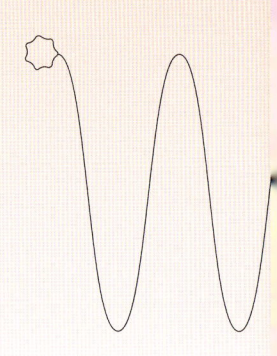

pedal · Tell Me a Story · culture

According to Retro Mechanical Labs, a recently discovered old Fox newsreel told the world that "archeologists had unearthed the original Electron Fuzz at the site of the worlds worst nuclear disaster. On December 23, 1949 nuclear engineers in charge of reactor safety were distracted when one of them built a guitar pedal from parts of the main reactor control panel. This guitar pedal caused massive distortion and led to massive, unimaginable destruction. This device lay buried under a pile of rubble and nuclear fallout until, after years of painstaking hard work, the Electron Fuzz was recovered and fully restored. We can finally hear the sound that caused that unforgettable apocalyptic day of destruction." RML makes high-gain distortion and fuzz pedals to order (Fallout Black or Nuclear Winter White), and they make up colorful myths to match.

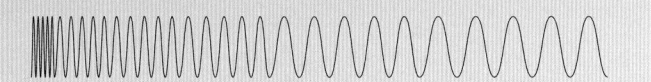

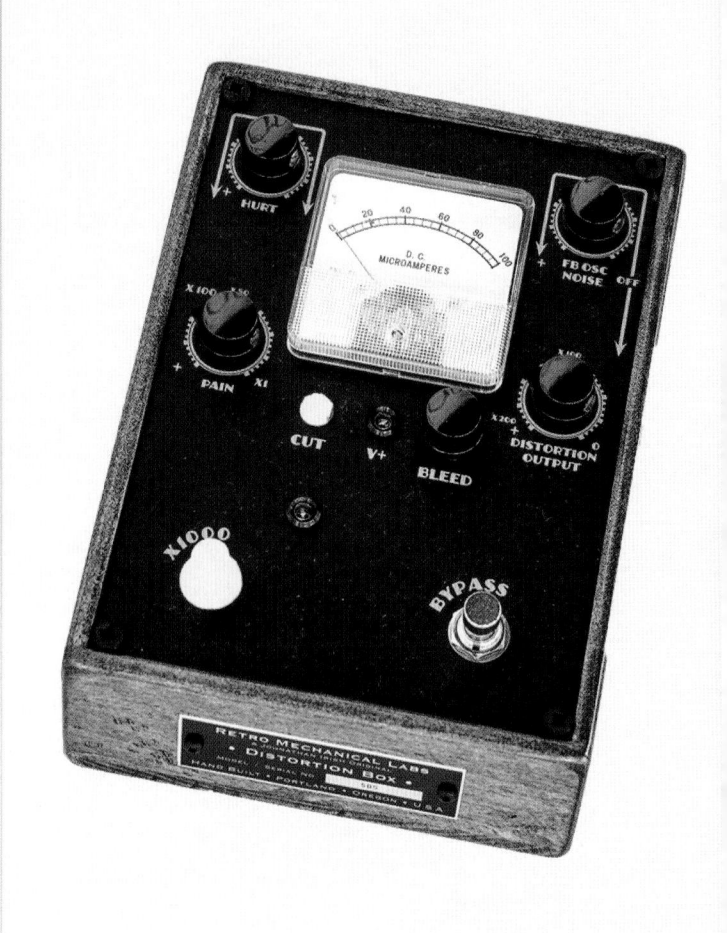

Electron Fuzz Custom Retro

Retro Mechanical Labs
2017
USA
Design: Johnathan Irish
Loan courtesy of Retro Mechanical Labs

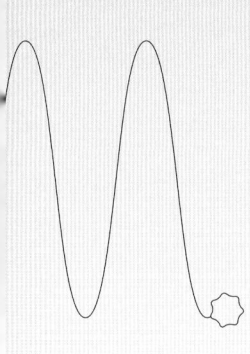

The namesake of this pedal is one John Wycliffe, a 14th-century dissident Catholic priest whose reformist politics ran afoul of the Pope. Declared a heretic, after his death Wycliffe was subjected to a final indignity of having his bones exhumed, burned and tossed in the river. It appears that arguing, as was Wycliffe's standard stump speech, that the Church give up all its property and the clergy live in poverty, was not well received among the powers of the day. "Turn up the gain, and your tone becomes a rich, raunchy wall of distortion. That seems fitting for the guy who first translated the Bible into English and had his bones burned by Rome 40 years later." So says Cody Fields, a South Carolina builder who hand-makes guitar effects pedals for church worship services.

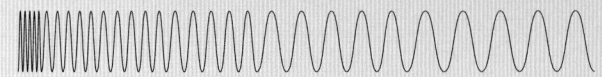

Wycliffe Fuzz

Westminster Effects
2017
USA
Design: Cody Fields
Numbered #7
Loan courtesy of Westminster Effects

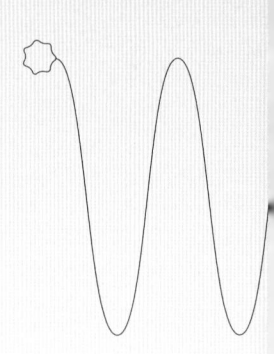

The moniker "Ponyboy" carries a dual meaning, at once named to reflect the Klon Centaur, the overdrive pedal which inspires its technical design and whose iconography becomes inverted in a beast's head placed on a boy's body, while also named after the central character in the acclaimed youth novel (and later movie), *The Outsiders*. The story of the Klon Centaur and the many clones ("klones") it inspires is told in a neighboring exhibit, "Surf 'n' Turf," where the Ponyboy pedal easily could be given a stall in the stable.

The action in the novel centers on Ponyboy and his best friend Johnny, two young teens on the run from the consequences of a youthful indiscretion that will turn them into adults. The story's theme is reflected in the Robert Frost poem "Nothing Gold Can Stay," read aloud by Ponyboy, an observation on the impermanence of youth and innocence. The book ends with the tragic but inevitable death of young Johnny, who in grand poetic gesture tells Ponyboy, "Stay gold." This wish, itself emblazoned on the tank top of the little Ponyboy figure on the pedal, conveys an alternate meaning in symbolizing the gold colored pedal enclosure of the Klon Centuar and the offshoot pedals (like the Ponyboy) it inspires. How can so much story be packed into one tiny enclosure?

Ponyboy Overdrive

Cheelee
2015
USA
Design: Peter Taylor
Signed by Peter Taylor, numbered #57 and dated 11-18-15
Curator's private collection

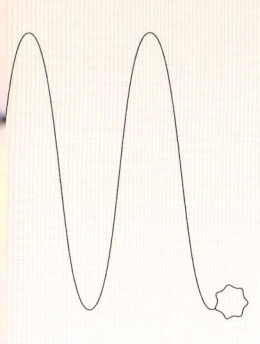

The artwork for this pedal has a personal story, and it involves two bellbottomed spangly dudes hanging out in London during the Swinging '60s. Fab, right? First is Jimi Hendrix, renowned for being soulful and psychedelic and sweetly disposed to helping others. Jimi took an immediate shine to this chap Alan Aldridge, the reigning illustrator and graphic artist of British rock royalty of the day, and asked Alan to decorate one of his Fender Stratocasters with some original designs. Tragically, Jimi died in 1970 before the art project could be realized, yet decades later the idea was resurrected when former Woodstock bandmate and guitarist Larry Lee asked Aldridge to adorn a black Strat Jimi had gifted him in 1969. Christened the JimiLee Mojo Guitar, this instrument serves as inspiration for The Flying-MOJO JimiLee fuzz-tone pedal, screenprinted with original Aldridge illustrations from the Stratocaster guitar. Reproduced on the pedal is a handwritten note from Jimi to Larry inviting him to record some music down in Nashville. This is one storied stompbox.

The JimiLee

Flying-MOJO
2015
USA
Art: Alan Aldridge
Loan courtesy of Flying-MOJO

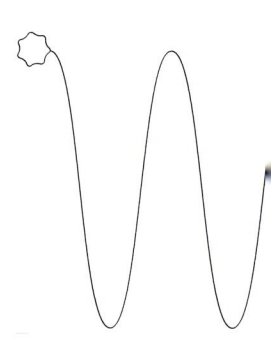

The word "mondegreen" refers to a misunderstood or misinterpreted word or phrase in a way that gives it a new meaning. In fact, according to author Sylvia Wright who coined the term, the definition implies that what is heard in the listener's mind is better than the original. "Mondegreen" comes from the 17th-century Scottish ballad "The Bonnie Earl o' Moray" where Wright misheard "and Lady Mondegreen" as the final words in the stanza "They have slain the Earl o' Moray, And laid him on the green." Wright said she always imagined the Earl dying beside his faithful lover "Lady Mondegreen," and found this an appealing, more romantic rendition of the story.

The Old Blood Noise Endeavors Mondegreen is a digital delay pedal "hell-bent on giving you something different than what you put in" owing to the added function of a modulation effect. As with any effects pedal, the guitarist always hopes what comes out of it is more pleasing to the ear than what went in.

Mondegreen Delay

Old Blood Noise Endeavors
2017
USA
Design: Seth McCarroll
Art: Jake Blanchard
Loan courtesy of Old Blood Noise Endeavors

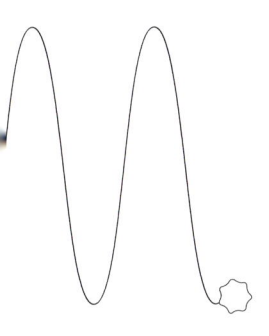

"In the outer recesses of space lays Zeta-6 quadrant's largest junkyard. Here, gravity-challenged junkers float about rubbing their rusted hulls together, while the sounds of these frictions reverberate into the worlds around them. Want your tone to sound like two abandoned spaceships crashing in the vacuum of space, their oxidized wings gnashing together and disintegrating into dust? With a wide gain range, the Frazz Dazzler pedal will frazzle dazzle you with its mean-spirited and aggressive fuzz whether you play guitar, bass or an electronic instrument." Words tell only half the story. As collateral materials go, the 2017 Dr. Scientist Web site was a world unto itself where animated graphics and a retro sci-fi mise-en-scéne did as much to tell the cosmic origins of each pedal as any words could hope to. Dr. Scientist pedals are designed and built by husband and wife team Ryan and Tanya Clarke whose cosmological musings emanate from the Okanagan Valley of British Columbia.

Frazz Dazzler

Dr. Scientist Sounds
2017
Canada
Design: Ryan Clarke
Art: Tanya Clarke
Loan courtesy of Dr. Scientist Sounds

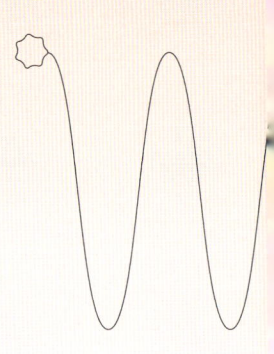

Naming a pedal after a place, either real or imagined, is an effective device for drawing associations between the sound of the pedal and some notable quality of place. This is particularly so for fuzz effects which may deliberately be harsh, aggressive and untamed. The Carcosa Fuzz has its own sound, and the name of a dark, mysterious, alien and possibly cursed place evokes the eerie sonics a fantasy might best convey. It's an effective metaphor.

The fictional city of Carcosa appears in the works of a number of authors, beginning with the Ambrose Bierce short story "An Inhabitant of Carcosa" (first published in a December, 1886 edition of the San Francisco Newsletter), and continuing in the popular horror stories of Robert W. Chambers and H. P. Lovecraft. In "An Inhabitant of Carcosa," a man wanders through a graveyard of several centuries past only to discover that he himself is dead, and amidst the ruins of the "ancient and famous city of Carcosa." In the recently completed television series "True Detective," Carcosa is presented as a temple located in the backwoods of Louisiana where ritualistic sexual abuse and murder of children have occurred. Aren't you glad you asked?

Carcosa Fuzz

DigiTech
2016
USA
Curator's private collection

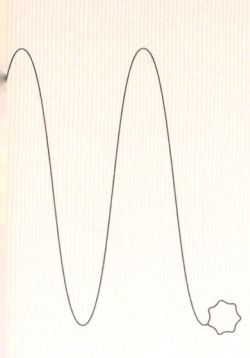

A Pedal Fo

Your Thoughts

⬡ Attack Release Filter (ARF)

Dwarfcraft
ca. 2015
USA
Design: Ben Hinz
Art: Iphigenia Douleur
Loan courtesy of Dwarfcraft Devices

Iphigenia Douleur (Foie Gras) is not yours, and never was.

Foie Gras:

"Girls Against Cat Calling" started as my own personal response to street harassment ... My aim is to teach young girls (and everyone else for that matter) ... that catcalling and other street harassment is unproductive and offensive.

Comment posted on an ARF pedal demonstration YouTube video:

I wouldn't buy anything with a whipped anti-men slogan on it. What's THAT got to do with music? NOTHING. You know what whipped is? -a guy who'd have woman's nagging printed right on his toys he uses when he's being a man and shouldn't be having to think about her made up objections about him being himself.

Dwarfcraft pedal builder Ben Hinz'response:

"Not Yours, Never Was" is a response to street harassment. Denying random knuckle draggers ownership over random women is not "anti-men" it's pro-woman, you ding dong. What does it have to do with music? A LOT. Women are a tiny minority in rock, and they are preyed upon relentlessly. Effects pedals are tools, and my tools are for equality. I would really suggest you try to think of women as human beings.

Iphigenia Douleur (Foie Gras) is a Los Angeles based designer and musician. She is a guitar driven, solo dronescapist. Listening to her music, she says, "is like giving yourself permission to indulge in something that is at once illicit, sacred, sacrilegious and startlingly rich." Douleur earned a B.S. in Visual Communication from SFSU and continues to produce art for her own pleasure and that of others.

The Mexica (Me-SHEE-Ka) indigenous people of Mexico and rulers of the Aztec Empire looked into the face of death everyday. La Calavera (the human skull) represented both the human sacrifice demanded by their cruel gods and the shedding of the human body at death, allowing for the glorious journey to dimensions known only to the gods. To that end, La Calavera Jamaica transports you from the depths of the Sea of Cortés with lush wet waves of undulating sound in Suave mode, to the heights of the Loco mode where dueling tones send you floating first into the dizzying stratosphere, then project you into outer space where you communicate with its inhabitants. Between these dimensions lives the Dinámica mode - earthbound yet superhuman. The performer controls the sound with strength and speed of his playing - using the man-made potion derived from the Jamaica flower to add the tart sweetness of the human touch. In this mode Carlos Santana plays atop the Templo Mayor pyramid in the Aztec capital of Tenochtitlan. Once he plugs La Calavera Jamaica into his guitar, it becomes the god Quetzalcoatl, a writhing feathered-serpent, whom he attempts to tame, appease, and worship, like death itself.

Guest written by Monica Cortés Viharo
Actor / Adjunct Professor, Theater Arts

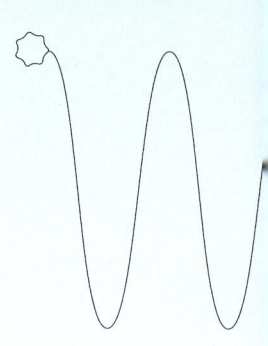

La Calavera (Jamaica edition)

Alexander Pedals
2015
USA
Design: Matthew Farrow
Loan courtesy of Alexander Pedals

A Pedal For Your Thoughts

Octapussy buzzes inside my brain like the perfectly blended cocktail, a Vesper in fact, potent and poetic, making me feel like James Bond leading a garage band, smooth 'n' stylish yet raw 'n' raunchy.

Like a bikini-clad biker chick riding a surfboard on a sonic shockwave of sensuality, notes swirl in the air while strangers dance together at a beach party.

Atomic sea monsters rise from the surf, eight notes above the sea and making raw, gurgling, discordant yet mesmerizing noises that permeate the atmosphere and cloud our consciousness like a thick marine mist.

At first the bestial cacophony is intimidating, menacing. Are they here to mangle or mingle, to hate or mate? But then the hypnotic effects of their reverberating riffs trigger deep and resonant chords within the darkest chambers of our primitive souls, and I am captivated, my mind a fuzzy purple haze.

Guest written by Will "the Thrill" Viharo
B movie maven, pulp fiction writer

OCTAPUSSY

Catalinbread Mechanisms of Music
2017
USA
Design: Howard Gee
Art: David Medel
Loan courtesy of Catalinbread Mechanisms of Music

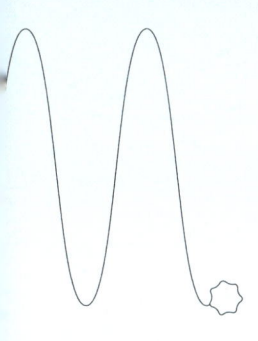

Psycho Flange

Not to mince words, the visual design of the Psycho Flange by Danelectro is a postmodern dumpster fire. Combining visual elements from the 1940s, '50s and '60s into a massively heavy metal enclosure, the contours vaguely resemble a three-eyed Art Deco owl. A hand-drawn swirl emanates from the foot switch (a visual theme borrowed from Alfred Hitchcock psychological thrillers á la Vertigo) implying this pedal will drive you truly insane. Strangely, the Psycho Flange also features a '60s style peace symbol between the printed graphics and control knobs. What is the designer trying to say about peace? What is the designer trying to say about insanity - or how they are connected? Could the Psycho Flange be a clue revealing a secret illuminati conspiracy? Or is it just a kitschy amalgam of retro-fetishism that means nothing at all?

Guest written by Ryan Burke
60 Cycle Hum: the guitar podcast

Throne Torcher

Pedals to the Metal is a foundational concept—no box-bolstered shredding on the big chords, no Metal, period. If the heavy Metal sound was originated by overdriving amps and speakers, guitar gear would be disposable—an ever-growing garage heaped with torn cones and smouldering circuitry. But

Psycho Flange

Danelectro
ca. 2001
USA
Loan courtesy of Ryan Burke

A Pedal For Your Thoughts

beyond the hellacious sound is the iconography of Metal, everything from Stonehenge to demented clowns, from vine-encrusted skulls to Viking hammers. Abominable Electronics, a boutique pedal purveyor in Durham, NC, has capitalized on this doom-driven symbology with an array of pedals sporting such titles as Hail Satan, Unholier Grail, and Hellmouth. The requisite demons embellish each metallic enclosure, blending devilish graphics with fuzz and volume knobs.

But none is more notorious than the Throne Torcher, a pedal associated with Varg Vikernes, the Black Metal musician, Nordic supremacist, and all-around jolly good felon. Vikernes was imprisoned for murdering Mayhem's guitarist Oystein Aarseth, and his sentence was increased for torching several Norwegian churches. The fact that Vikernes again roams the streets may be troubling to some.

The original Throne Torcher has a B&W graphic of a church enveloped by raging flames and above the steeple, a cloaked demon leers at the fiery inferno. The newest edition of the pedal opts for a hideous skulled demon devouring the steeple, eyes flashing red while creeping flames lick at the church's siding. Punch in this pedal during a solo and you've got the devil to play.

Guest written by Steve Seid
Emeritus Curator, Berkeley Art Museum

Throne Torcher

Abominable Electronics
2017
USA
Design: Patrick Emmons
Art: Matt Kerley
Loan courtesy of Abominable Electronics

Fuzzy Muff

Petting Zoo

Let's start with the original Big Muff Pi, a 1969 effects pedal that was the first of many Big Muff versions produced by pedal maker Electro-Harmonix. In the hands of Pink Floyd's David Gilmour, King Crimson's Robert Fripp and quite a few other guitar virtuosos the Big Muff quickly caught on and became one of the most popular guitar effects pedals of all time.

There's no hiding from the Big Muff. This is as blatant a metaphor as you're likely to find in the entire etymology of guitar pedals, yet strangely it's the elephant in the room that defies acknowledgement. It's the adolescent in every guitarist, the prefrontal cortex that refuses to grow up. "Big Muff Pi" contains not one - but two! - different euphemisms for female genitalia, and is a play on "fuzz" as a colorful graphic metaphor for the pubic territories. The implications of the name, and its obvious anatomical reference, spawned a world of offspring - fuzzy variants with similarly suggestive names like Muff Diver, Large Beaver and the Hairpie Classic. You'll find some lively examples on display along with a few highly graphic ones, too (thus, the "peep" curtain).

What do we make of all this? Men might be tempted to muffle 50 years of adolescent self-indulgence, or women to vent about the indignities of objectification, but perhaps if we engage in a bit of semiotic deconstruction we can achieve a more sympathetic relationship to the sexual reference represented by the Big Muff and its descendants. So, what possible origin myths might this reveal?

○ Rock music's debt to the blues is deep and seminal and reveals a profound connection between American popular and African-American music traditions. Life is lived openly and without shame in the blues, and sexual innuendo and colorful sexual euphemisms are pervasive storytelling devices. With countless references to the power of "jelly roll" controlling many a romantic relationship, and the highly suggestive "I need a little finger in my bowl," a woman's sexuality is never denied. Does this perhaps pave the way for names like the Big Muff, the Cream Puff, and the Dirty Beaver as being no more inappropriate in the world of rock than the raucous off-color euphemisms wailing from the blues juke joints that preceded them?

○ As the female organ of sexual union and procreation, the "muff" represents the regenerative impulse and serves as a metaphor for the act of creation. What better metaphor for making music than a potent fertility symbol?

○ In light of the ancient Greek prophet Tiresias' claim that women experience nine times the sexual pleasure of men, is it any wonder that men might succumb to a condition of "pussy envy" – a mirror image reflection of the psychological construct of penis envy – given form in the fuzz of the Big Muff?

○ Although marketed as a fuzz effect, Electro-Harmonix founder Mike Matthews claims his actual intent for the Big Muff was to lengthen the sustain of a plucked guitar string, thus achieving a "sweet violin like sound" and a highly desirable effect in musical performance. In her book *Feminine Endings* (2002), musicologist Susan McClary talks explicitly about the place of music as a metaphor for sexual activity, claiming that while some music seeks climax in driving forward toward a goal (in the masculine), other music strives for a state of sustained pleasure (with the feminine). Is any device more appropriately named for sustaining musical notes (and sensual pleasure) than the "Big Muff"?

Notes from the nether regions . . .

Big Muff Pi
This recent issue Big Muff Pi is a good facsimile of the box that started it all. Fifty years of puns, graphic metaphors and not so thinly veiled allusions owe their inspiration to the original EHX Big Muff.

Merkin
The manufacturer's own promotional copy reads, "A fuzzy cover-up for your bare pudenda. Look it up." The Art Nouveau style typography does double-duty in a most delightful way, creating an overall effect of nothing so much as an appearance by the 1960s Dick Tracy comic strip character, The Brush.

⬢ Big Muff Pi

Electro-Harmonix
2017
USA
Design: Bob Myer, Mike Matthews
Loan courtesy of Electro-Harmonix

⬢ Merkin

Catalinbread Mechanisms of Music
2015
USA
Design: Howard Gee
Art: David Medel
Curator's private collection

✱ Super Hard On

ZVEX Effects
2016
USA
Design: Zachary Vex
Hand-painted enclosure, signed & numbered #K083 (7-14-16)
Loan courtesy of ZVEX Effects

✱ Muffuletta

JHS Pedals
2015
USA
Design: Josh Scott, Jon Cusack
Hand-painted enclosure
Loan courtesy of JHS Pedals

Fuzzy Muff Petting Zoo

Super Hard On

ZVEX figured out a long time ago the most effective way to pound a Big Muff fuzz into screaming ecstasy is with a Super Hard On, a boost with more thrust.

Muffuletta

On display is a hand-painted version of the JHS Muffuletta in which the technical design of a Big Muff gets rebranded as an aromatic mouth-watering sandwich. Euphemistically speaking, "muffuletta" imparts a succulent quality to anything that stands to be devoured.

Fur Coat Fuzz

Just like in naming, often the graphic content of Muff-style pedals is not what you think it is, with the meaning lying just beneath the surface. The image on the Fur Coat Fuzz is a masquerade, playing dress up where maybe a good dressing down is what's called for. Despite its skeletal features, this pedal displays an anatomically correct representation of fuzz and all the rest.

⬢ Fur Coat Fuzz

Orange Pedals
2017
England
Loan courtesy of Orange USA

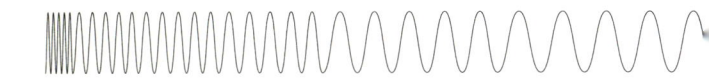

If we were to award one pedal for distinctive art direction, the Fig Fumb would be a high contender with its charming 1920s *Steamboat Willie* cartoon-style illustration. This effects pedal, in the words of the builder, allows guitarists "to dial in perfect muff tones from all the different flavours of the various Big Muff eras." But do we even give a fig? While Elizabethan literature establishes "fig" as a small, valueless thing, in Greek and Italian the word for fig can be slang for "vulva," seemingly due to the appearance of a ripe fig when split wide open.

✿ Fig Fumb

Stone Deaf Effects & Amplification
2017
England
Loan courtesy of Stone Daeaf Effects

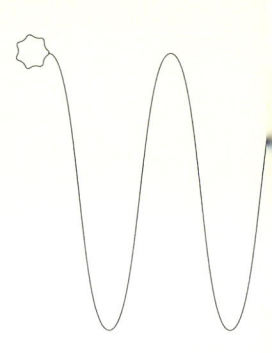

In the company Web site, pedal builder Fran Blanche provocatively asks, "Chick Pedal?" before declaring "A unique tone contour gives this fuzz a puffy, fluffy, broad, thick sound. The deceptively edible motif uses white retro knobs and is topped off by a super cute Pink LED!" In lecture, Fran says, "the Cream Puff was inspired by a Hostess Snowball: a coconut covered, pink, artificial snowball." We note that Fran worked for Electro-Harmonix and designed the NYC Big Muff (Muff v.9) in 1999-2000. In Fran's hands, the Cream Puff is a decidedly feminine looking object which wouldn't look out of place on a woman's dressing table. Is a fluffy Puff like a Big Muff?

Cream Puff ✦

Frantone Electronics
2017
USA
Design: Fran Blanche
Loan courtesy of Frantone Electronics

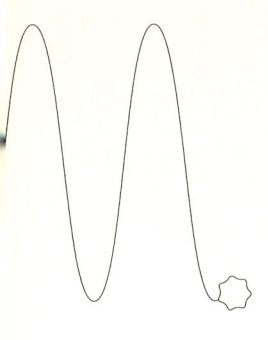

♣ Dirty Beaver Ram's Head

Wilson Effects
2017
USA
Art: David Medel
Loan courtesy of Wilson Effects

♣ Pussy Power

Cioks
2017
Denmark
Design: Poul Ciok
Loan courtesy of Cioks

Dirty Beaver Ram's Head

Relevant etymology: Wilson's the builder, "Ram's Head" is an early version of the Big Muff, and "Dirty Beaver" is best left to the imagination. Or not.

Pussy Power

Pink and proud, the Pussy Power is a bastion of empowerment, providing power to all the pedals on a guitarist's pedalboard. The display unit was specially built for the PedalCulture exhibition with a continuously lit power indicator light serving as a burning beacon of sensory pleasure.

Swollen Pickle

You didn't think you were really going to get off the schoolyard without someone dropping trow and exposing this pedal, did you? It, too, has fuzz.

⬣ Swollen Pickle

Way Huge
2016
USA
Loan courtesy of Dunlop Manufacturing

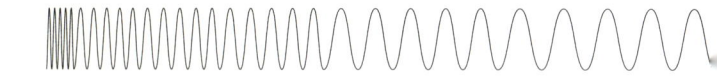

Tones of

pedal

the Gods

In the quest for sublime tone guitarists like to talk about the "tone in their head" - but really, they're often chasing someone else's tone. In this exhibit we find a selection of pedals laying claim to the signature guitar sounds of iconic rock guitarists - often conflated with some version of the Holy Grail - literally indexed to specific recordings, eras and musical performances. With particular reference to the recently departed, these pedals are designed to reproduce a fair approximation of heaven on earth. Just add signal and, like a freeze-dried meal, one hopes for magic, not mush. An essential element in this equation is recorded music, as personal recollection and live performance mean little in the quest for tone without a tangible reference to immortalize, a fact to which the pedals in this exhibit attest.

The zeal with which modern-day guitarists chase legendary guitar tones has led to a significant amount of self-awareness among guitarists as to the fervor of their quest - often resulting in a heavy dose of irony heaped upon the sacramental journey to tonal bliss. In the clichéd argument that "tone is in the fingers," the opposing position might be that tone is in the toes (i.e. stompboxes). Thus, in what amounts to a sly cultural meme, we are blessed with a YouTube video of a re-edit from the 2004 movie *Downfall* in which the monologue of Adolph Hitler's seething, maniacal rant is reinterpreted with newly installed subtitles. Hitler berates his core officers, summoning the furies for their refusal to accept that guitarist Stevie Ray Vaughn could possibly achieve such sublime tone without plugging into the legendary Ibanez Tubescreamer overdrive pedal. Hitler, too, is looking for his stairway to heaven.

Guitarists have been using distortion for effect practically since the invention of electronic amplification, but it is the Maestro FZ-1 Fuzz-Tone that has the distinction of being the first commercially available fuzz effect. This device was a product of the early '60s Nashville country music scene where, in a moment of legendary serendipity, audio engineer Glen T. Snoddy would design the effect after first hearing fuzzy distortion coming from a damaged mixing console! The 1962 Gibson patent application for the FZ-1 says the device was intended for stringed instruments "to produce tones simulating other instruments such as trumpets, trombones and tubas." (You can hear the FZ-1 simulated horns on a demonstration phonograph record released at the time.) As a commercial entity, fuzz fizzled until Keith Richards employed a Maestro fuzz driven guitar tone in "(I Can't Get No) Satisfaction." The song took over the radio airwaves during the summer of 1965, blasting from transistor radios on lawns and beaches everywhere. Wanna go back in time? Look at the graphic design of the Satisfaction pedal, it's a 45 RPM record with center hole insert adapting the disc for playing on a standard turntable of the era. Interesting to note, "Keef" used an effects pedal only one other time in his entire recording career.

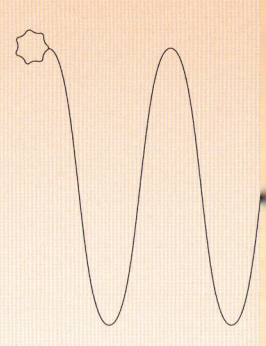

Satisfaction

Electro-Harmonix
2017
USA
Loan courtesy of Electro-Harmonix

Tones of the Gods

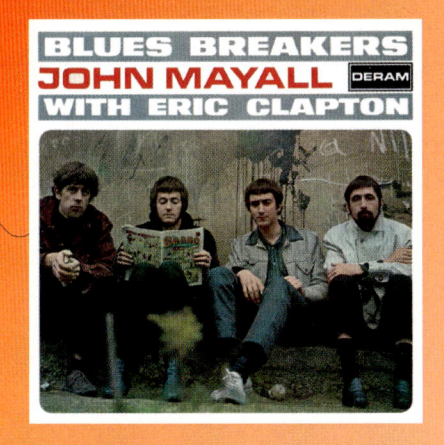

Ever feel like you need a boost? Guitarists do! Functionally speaking, a boost pedal magnifies the strength of a guitar's output feeding into an amplifier. The AnalogMan Beano Boost is based on the 1960s British Dallas Rangemaster effects pedal which was known for enhancing treble frequencies, serving as many a guitarist's secret weapon in driving a British Vox amp into a sizzling distorted sound. The Rangemaster is strongly associated with guitarists of '60s British blues and rock such as Brian May (Queen), Marc Bolan (T. Rex), and Ritchie Blackmore (Deep Purple), but never more closely than in the "John Mayall Blues Breakers with Eric Clapton" album (1966). The name "Beano" derives from the name of the comic strip Clapton is seen reading on the album cover, nicknamed the "Beano" album for obvious reason.

Beano Boost

AnalogMan
2017
USA
Design: Mike Piera
Loan courtesy of AnalogMan

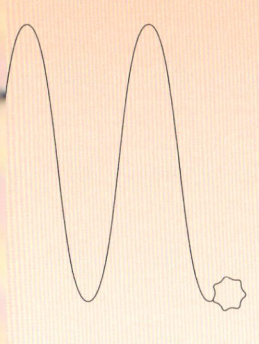

From the shop of Jim Dunlop: "Over the course of '69-'70, Jimi Hendrix appeared at his most noted live appearances-Live at Woodstock, Live at Berkeley, and Live at the Fillmore East-using a mysterious red Fuzz Face Distortion with white knobs. That fuzz box sounded like a completely different animal from any of the other Fuzz Face pedals in Jimi's arsenal, snarling with a far more aggressive, biting tone. The pedal itself has been lost to history, but its unmistakably unique tone lives on in the recordings of those three iconic shows, and Hendrix aficionados have tried to cop that sound for years. We are happy to say that their tonal quest can finally come to a glorious end. Poring tirelessly over all of the different customized circuit designs Jimi used over the years, our engineers narrowed down this elusive fuzz tone to a version of the [Roger Mayer] Octavia circuit that didn't have the octave up signal." Tone of the gods, indeed.

Jimi Hendrix Gypsy Fuzz

Dunlop Manufacturing
2017
USA
Art: Gered Mankowitz
Loan courtesy of Dunlop Manufacturing

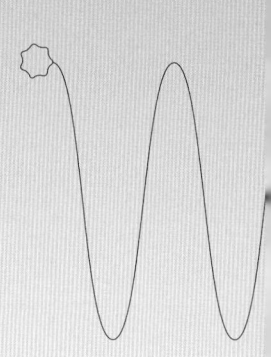

The legendary guitarist Jimi Hendrix burst upon the world stage at the Monterey Pop Festival in 1967, and rock music was forever changed. While Jimi's artistry, style, and showmanship (not to mention heart and spirit) have all contributed to his singular standing in the history of popular music, there's also something to be said for Jimi's use of technology. Jimi eagerly adopted and applied the very latest musical effects made available to him - and in brilliantly creative ways - by working collaboratively with Britain's virtuoso sound engineer Roger Mayer. Use of fuzz, octave, vibe, wah, and rotary speaker propelled Hendrix to heights of personally creative musical expression unmatched by most other guitarists in rock 'n' roll. These effects, plus phasing and tremolo, are found in the Keeley Electronics Monterey Rotary Fuzz Vibe pedal. No one claims this box will have you seeing God, but in the right hands the colors of the palette are yours to glow like Jimi at Monterey.

Monterey Rotary Fuzz Drive

Keeley Electronics
2017
USA
Loan courtesy of Keeley Electronics

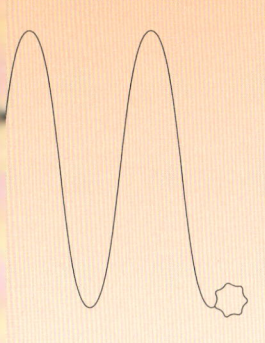

The Binson Echorec was notable for strange, lush atmospherics that lent themselves perfectly to the haunting and ethereal psychedelic stylings of mid-'60s rock. Using digital emulation, the Catalinbread pedal design resurrects the Echorec's legendary soundscape originally achieved via a multi-head steel drum design employing varying degrees of echo, repeat and swell to whatever signal fed into it. If there's one band that fully took advantage of the Echorec it was Pink Floyd in its most experimental and psychedelic '60s phase. The distinctive playing styles of original Pink Floyd guitarist Syd Barrett and his replacement David Gilmour are largely associated with this effect used on countless Floyd songs beginning in 1968. At the 1971 Pompeii outing captured on film the band seems keyed up by the surreal beauty of their surroundings, and there's an exploratory edge to their playing that is soon to be lost in their transition to megastardom.

Echorec

Catalinbread Mechanisms of Music
2017
USA
Design: Nicholas Harris, Howard Gee, Jack Pineda
Loan courtesy of Catalinbread Mechanisms of Music

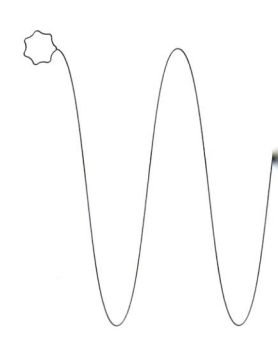

Keeley's Memphis Sun is named after the most legendary rock 'n' roll recording studio of all time, Memphis Sun Studios. Arguably the first rock and roll single, Jackie Brenston and his Delta Cats' "Rocket 88" was recorded there in 1951 with song composer Ike Turner on keyboards, leading the studio to claim status as the birthplace of rock 'n' roll. On this hallowed ground, owner Sam Phillips made the earliest recordings of Elvis, and recorded music legends Jerry Lee Lewis, Carl Perkins, Roy Orbison, Johnny Cash and a lengthy who's who of rock, country, rockabilly and R & B talent.

It's the room, man, it's the room! Inspired by the legendary acoustic properties of the Sun recording studio and period-correct audio gear, this pedal simulates vintage tones of the 1950s with lo-fi reverb and slapback echo, and a not quite period correct double-tracking feature. Who said time travel isn't possible?

Memphis Sun

Keeley Electronics
2017
USA
Loan courtesy of Keeley Electronics

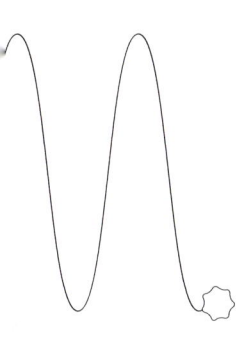

In 1970 Led Zeppelin took the stage of London's venerated Royal Albert Hall and delivered one of the most celebrated gigs of their career. Jimmy Page's Gibson Les Paul guitar and custom Hiwatt amps outputting to Marshall speaker cabinets filled the entire hall with sound, says Catalinbread, with a "cornucopia of colors at levels ranging from a mouse whisper to rave ups louder than a jumbo jet taking off only inches over your head." This live performance, according to one reviewer, "completely destroyed the ever-weakening argument about British reserve . . . [with] electricity ... building up throughout the evening."

The band agreed to have the evening filmed for a (never released) TV special, then finally, in 2003, a publicly released DVD gave Catalinbread the audio reference it needed to pack the Jimmy Page guitar and amp tones into the RAH overdrive pedal. Jimmy Page tones from January 9, 1970 at Royal Albert Hall: Your wish is our command.

🟢 RAH

Catalinbread Mechanism of Music
2017
USA
Design: Howard Gee
Graphic Artist: David Medel
Loan courtesy of Catalinbread Mechanism of Music

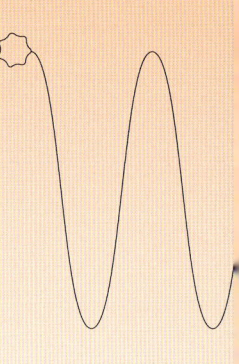

The Dreamscape is a multi-modulation (chorus, flanger, vibrato) effects pedal designed around the signature clean tones of John Petrucci. Petrucci, a founding member of the progressive metal band Dream Theater, was ranked the 17th greatest guitarist of all time in a 2012 Guitar World magazine reader's poll.

TC Electronic's TonePrint technology is one of the new technologies with a digital user interface permitting a pedal user to internally customize a vast range of tone settings. The manufacturer adds value to its products by inviting "rock royalty" to custom design their own tone settings and making these settings available for download by consumers. Taken to its logical conclusion is The Dreamscape, offering six signature tones personally designed by John Petrucci and blessing the ardent fan with these very tones for his own rig.

The Dreamscape

TC Electronic
2017
Denmark
Design: Tore Lynggard Mogensen, John Petrucci
Loan courtesy of TC Electronic

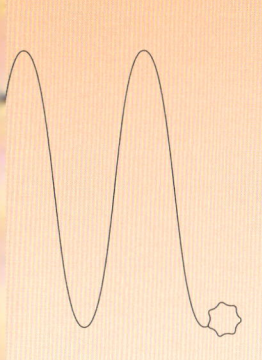

The Crossroads effects pedal is positioned as the definitive statement of Clapton mojo in a box. The manufacturer worked with Eric Clapton and his long-time guitar tech Lee Dickson in the digital modeling of speaker cabinets, microphones with their placement, guitar effects, and audio engineering to re-create seven signature Clapton tones in one pedal. From songs like "Badge" with its swirling rotary speaker, to "Layla" (Unplugged) with its intimate acoustic tone, to "Sunshine of Your Love" which features Eric's signature "woman tone," DigiTech says "Crossroads spans 30 years of Clapton culture and tone."

"Cross Road Blues" (or "Crossroads") is a 1936 song by the legendary blues artist Robert Johnson. It was recorded live by Cream - the "super group" consisting of bassist Jack Bruce, drummer Ginger Baker, and Eric Clapton - at Winterland, on March 10, 1968. The performance venue sat at the intersection of Post and Steiner, near San Francisco's Japantown, in a 1928 building which had presented opera, been an ice skating rink and served as a boxing arena. In the 1960s, Winterland was affiliated with Bill Graham's Fillmore Auditorium.

Crossroads

DigiTech
ca. 2005
USA
Design: Tom Cram
Loan courtesy of Eric C. Ness

97

pedal culture

Curator's documentation

pedal culture

Curator's documentation

Credits

Joshua Singer
Gallery Director, DESIGNSPACE
School of Design, SFSU

Ronald Light
Guest Curator

Exhibition Design
Julia Bulger
Michael Capulong
Maya Chastain
Megan Chen
Nicolas Corona
Dominic Decarlo
Amena Elmashni
Jenyce Garay
Lizzy Johnson
Monica Lira
Mary Jo Lonsdale
Maggie Nguyen
Ashley Pae
Sonny Pham
AJ Plummer
Erica Rigney
Ashley Velasquez
Audrey Walker

Design & installation assistance
Craig Lloyd
Kenan Shapero

pedal culture

Exhibition Photography
Jeff Spirer

Additional Photography
I, Maker
Kerri Leslie

Guest Commentary
Ryan Burke
Steve Seid
Monica Cortes Viharo
Will Viharo

Music Performance
Jimmy Leslie

Exhibition Sponsors
Guitar Player Magazine
Pedal Genie

Additional Support
Casa Sanchez SF

**Project Funding for PedalCulture
Was Provided by an Anonymous Donor**

Credits

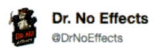

Dr. No Effects
@DrNoEffects

The curator of San Fransisco's Pedal Culture expo concidered my craft as art @AlainJohannes 11:11 pedal will be displayed there!

9:09 AM - 1 Sep 2017

4 Retweets 32 Likes

It is fully ridiculous that a #farmpedals #highpassboost is hanging out in this company at the SFSU Designspace Pedal Culture exhibit in San Fransisco…..... #spruceeffects #ehx

7 ♥ 159   11:37 PM Nov 9, 2017

pedal   Exhibition Credits   culture
                              102

pedal culture

We extend the greatest of gratitude for pedal loans to:

Abominable Electronics / Patrick Emmons
Alexander Pedals
AnalogMan
Beetronics
Ryan Burke
Catalinbread Mechanisms Of Music
Cioks
Dr. No Effects
Dr. Scientist
Dunlop Manufacturing
Dwarfcraft Devices
Electro-Harmonix
Farm Pedals
Flying-MOJO
Frantone Electronics
Joe Gore
IdiotBox Effects

JHS Pedals
Keeley Electronics
Eric C. Ness
Old Blood Noise Endeavors
Orange Pedals
Pedal Genie
Rainger FX / David Rainger
Real Guitars
Retro Mechanical Labs / Johnathan Irish
Roland Corporation U.S.
Spruce Effects / Brian Bicknell and
    Katie Morgan
Stone Deaf Effects & Amplification
SviSound
TC Electronic
Wampler Pedals
Westminster Effects
Wilson Effects
Wren and Cuff
Wrought Iron Leather and Effects
ZVEX

Exhibition Credits

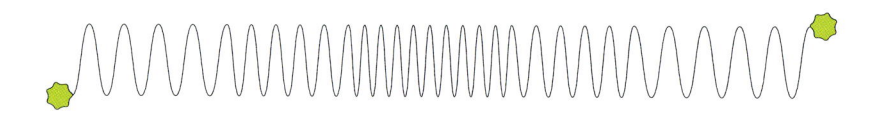

Ronald Light, in the words of George Lois, is a cultural provocateur. Ron had a varied career developing innovative and influential programs in arts, culture and technology - often in service to very human needs for personal and community development. He has a B.A. in anthropology from San Francisco State University and an MFA in design from California Institute of the Arts. Ron lives in San Francisco where he plays guitar, badly.

Megan Pai is a graphic designer from San Diego, currently pursuing a degree in Architecture at Princeton University. Her entrance into the creative realm was marked by hours spent in a darkroom, printing portraits of her mom and suburbia. Today, her photographic work persists in the form of low-contrast shots of the quiet things in life: glowing lamps, spilt milk, and people mid-yawn. This documentary mode of preserving transient times informs her desire to produce anomalous yet enduring editorial designs.

Jeff Spirer is a photographer and writer currently residing in Lisbon, Portugal. Once a photographer of professional prize fights, Jeff's best known for bringing a rock'n'roll sensibility to shooting vivid images of live performance featuring punk, goth, metal, fetish and burlesque alternative cultures. He has exhibited in gallery and corporate settings and published in sports and music publications including Guitar Player and Drum! Magazine.

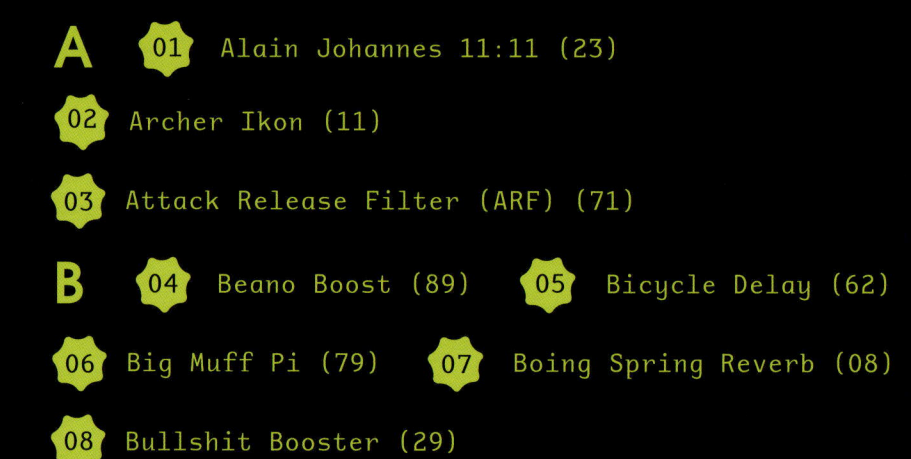

Index

A
- 01 Alain Johannes 11:11 (23)
- 02 Archer Ikon (11)
- 03 Attack Release Filter (ARF) (71)

B
- 04 Beano Boost (89)
- 05 Bicycle Delay (62)
- 06 Big Muff Pi (79)
- 07 Boing Spring Reverb (08)
- 08 Bullshit Booster (29)

pedal culture

C
- 09 La Calavera (72)
- 10 Carcosa Fuzz (69)
- 11 Centaur (10)
- 12 Charlie Fuzz (27)
- 13 Cream Puff (83)
- 14 Crossroads (96)

D
- 15 Dirty Beaver Ram's Head (84)
- 16 The Dracarys (31)
- 17 The Dreamscape (95)
- 18 Dr FREAKENSTEIN FUZZ DRFF-3LE (25)
- 19 Duh Remedial Fuzz (14)

Index

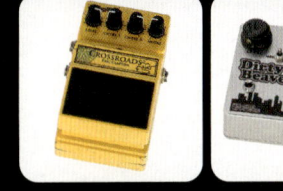

pedal culture

E 20 Echorec (92)   21 Echozoid (18)   22 Electron Fuzz Custom Retro (63)

F 23 FDR-1 '65 Deluxe Reverb (07)   24 Fig Fumb (82)   25 Frazz Dazzler (68)
  26 FRV-1 '63 Fender Reverb (07)   27 Fur Coat Fuzz (81)

H 28 Hall of Fame 2 (58)   29 High Pass Boost (16)   30 Holy Wahcamoly (37)

I 31 Irkalla Manifest Fuzz (28)   **J** 32 Jimi Hendrix Gypsy Fuzz (90)
  33 The JimiLee (66)

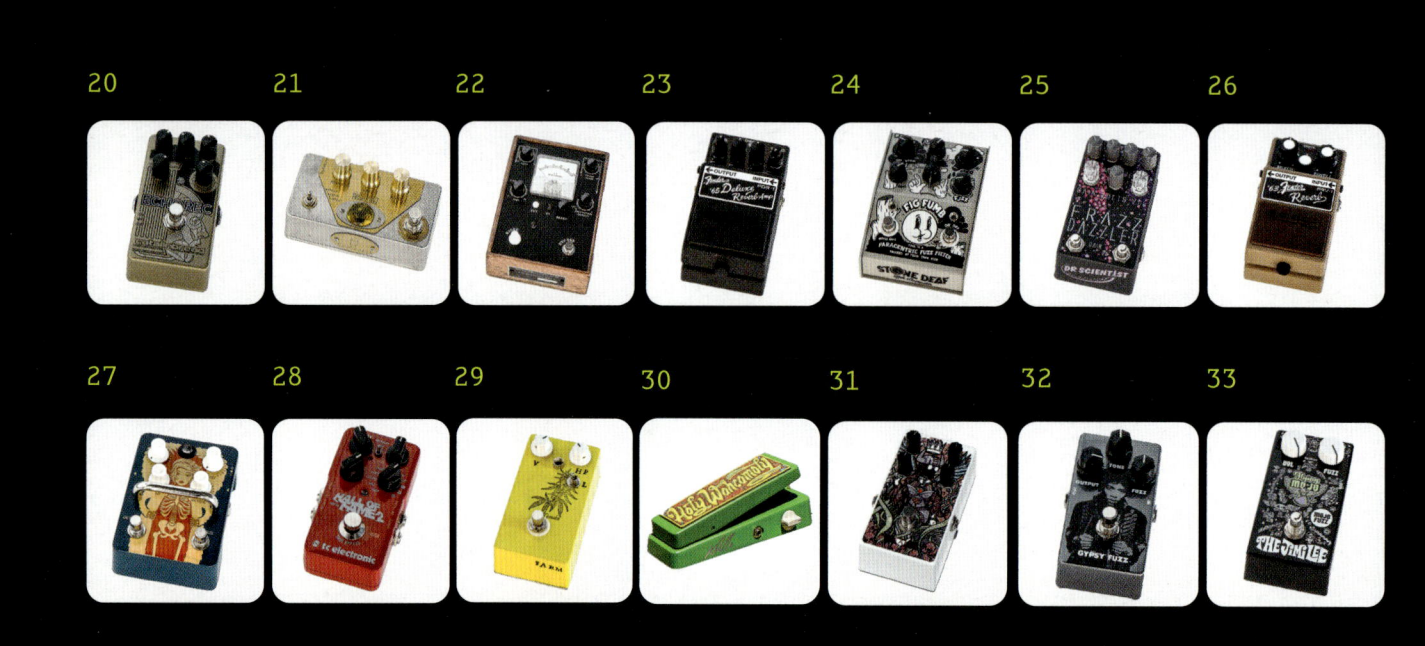

Index

pedal culture

K 34 Klon Klone (10)   35 Kongpressor (26)   **M** 36 Memphis Sun (93)

37 Merkin (79)   38 Miku Stomp (32)   39 Mondegreen Delay (67)

40 Monterey Rotary Fuzz Drive (91)   41 Muffuletta (80)   **O** 42 OctaHive (20)

43 OCTAPUSSY (73)   44 Old Growth Fuzz (15)   45 Orcist Overdrive (17)

P 46 Ponyboy Overdrive (65)   47 Psycho Flange (74)   48 Pussy Power (84)

Index
109

R
- 49 RAH (94)
- 50 Roadkiller (30)
- 51 Road Runner Octave FuzzWah (21)
- 52 Ron Fucking Swanson Fuzz (33)

S
- 53 Satisfaction (88)
- 54 Spring King Reverb (09)
- 55 Spring Theory (08)
- 56 Super Hard On (80)
- 57 Swollen Pickle (85)

T
- 58 Throne Torcher (75)
- 59 Topanga (09)
- 60 Troy Van Leeuwen "TVL" Octavia (22)
- 61 Tumnus (11)

W
- 62 The WARTHOG Distortion (19)
- 63 Wycliffe Fuzz (64)

Index
110

pedal · Index 111 · culture